Drawing upon the wisdom o
Edwards in particular, Johr
size-fits-all' approach to sanc
much of evangelical teaching to lay out a more biblical
and wise path toward Godliness. Any Christian who
wants to think deeply about the normal Christian life and
what it means to 'struggle successfully' will benefit from
the practical insights found in these pages.

Bradley Aucoin
Pastor, Christ Covenant Church,
Baton Rouge, Los Angeles

Intimacy with God, by Dr. John Hannah, will encourage
and disturb you. As only a seasoned Christ-following
scholar can do, Hannah probes the question: 'How
does one walk with God?' To Hannah, the answer is
not formulaic; it is found in following a personalized,
time-intensive journey with the Creator. This book will
rescue you from a self-help, quick-fix, perspective, and
yet challenge you to follow Christ practically in old and
bold ways—all while believing the best is yet to come.

Mark Yarbrough
President, Professor of Bible Exposition,
Dallas Theological Seminary, Dallas, Texas

What a blessing to have been a student of John Hannah!
Sitting in his classroom was like trekking through
mountain ranges, the majesty of the living God on display
all around, glorious vistas opening up in the words of
his lectures. I'm delighted that this book will make
Dr. Hannah's teaching available beyond his classroom,
and I'm eager to keep copies on hand to give it away to
anyone seeking a more intimate walk with God.

James M. Hamilton
Professor of Biblical Theology, The Southern Baptist
Theological Seminary, Louisville, Kentucky

It is rare to find a book on cultivating a life with God that is so deeply grounded in theology, so honest about the everyday realities of Christian living, and so free of the type of formulaic approach that occupies far too many books on spiritual life. *Intimacy with God* clearly flows out of a lifetime spent not only in studying and teaching what the Scriptures and great Christians of the past have to teach us about deep things of God, but in pursuing a growing intimacy with Him. I especially appreciate the way John Hannah draws on hymns throughout the book to remind readers that in God's presence there is 'fullness of joy, at His right hand there are pleasures forever!' (Ps. 16:11).

Timothy D. Hall
Dean, Howard College of Arts and Sciences, Samford University, Birmingham, Alabama

Intimacy
with God

A PRACTICAL GUIDE
IN OUR STRUGGLES

John D. Hannah

CHRISTIAN
FOCUS

Scripture quotations are taken from the *New American Standard Bible®*, Copyright © 1960, 1962, 1963, 1968, 1971, 1972, 1973, 1975, 1977, 1995 by The Lockman Foundation Used by Permission. (www.Lockman.org)

Copyright © John D. Hannah 2020

paperback ISBN 978-1-5271-0555-3
epub ISBN 978-1-5271-0624-6
mobi ISBN 978-1-5271-0625-3

10 9 8 7 6 5 4 3 2 1

Published in 2020
by
Christian Focus Publications Ltd,
Geanies House, Fearn, Ross-shire,
IV20 1TW, Great Britain.
www.christianfocus.com

Cover design by Pete Barnsley
Printed by Bell & Bain, Glasgow

MIX
Paper from
responsible sources
FSC
www.fsc.org
FSC® C007785

Contents

INTRODUCTION

I do not think my religious experience was at all unique in most ways. I was nurtured in the Christian faith within a fairly solid, orthodox church, having come to Christ as a pre-teen. The initial years of understanding the claims and accomplishments of Christ were not spectacular events for me. I enjoyed the gatherings for worship, the instruction in the faith by a devout, godly Sunday School teacher – the man most influential in speaking of Christ to me (as well as many other things as I worked for him in the construction trade and he became a surrogate father to me in my teenage years). I was uniquely shaped by the corporate prayer meetings where I found acceptance and love as a follower of Jesus. I also loved the unique times of fellowship with God and my new-found family.

Typical of many, I suppose, in my late high school years I discovered that my conduct was not always congruent with my head and my profession of redemption. My walk did not consistently reflect my talk and a crisis loomed like a dark cloud over the horizon of my life. The answer in typical evangelical parlance to my realization was the need for a dedicatory experience of surrendering my life, departing from preoccupations with dark shadows. I had to rededicate myself to Christ at the foot of Calvary to begin a new life of submission to God. In the midst of my religious turmoil, I was instructed that I needed to come to grips with Romans 12:1-2, a text described to me as a once-for-all-time decision that would bring solace to my troubled soul (I do not doubt that it did, but it was not as durative as I was led to believe). I was then taught that I would need to maintain a consistent state of mental, emotional, and religious devotion toward God in order to have such a wonderful and elevated state of spirituality, that not only dedication but constancy were the keys to a victorious walk with God.

Years have passed in my cycle of life experiences (education, marriage, children, a professional career as a religious educator, the aging process, grandchildren, and now the ultimate graying years) and I have become skeptical of some of my earlier instruction in Christian living. While I found much richness from my teachers, I found that the form of instruction I had received was more a psychological approach than a real one. 'If I believe I am ok, then I am ok,' 'If I have constancy and intensity of faith, all is well,' seemed to have been the messages I had embraced, though they were enshrined in biblical texts and religious clichés.

In short, I found myself in a far more complex world than I had surmised to exist when it came to the issue of obedience and conformity to God. 'What does it mean to walk with God?' I asked when sincerity of intent did not produce the fruit of consistency. Am I doomed to consistent failure, unable to invoke the right management technique? Is walking with God being blind to the darkness in my soul, the places where the light of the gospel shines less brightly? How is the discrepancy between my private life and the life people see to be explained?

If I had a ticker tape on my forehead revealing the thoughts of my heart, would I have as many friends? If the spiritual life can be compared to the art of juggling, it would seem that I could learn to deal with three balls; however, what do I do when life is composed of ten or twenty balls? It seems that in this world of complexity, I found that some of the 'balls' – some areas of my moral and intellectual life – were bouncing all over the floor.

If the spiritual life could be compared to flying an aircraft, it would be comparatively easy, I suppose, if there were only one or two buttons to push to take off and to land. However, what if there are numerous buttons and a great degree of situational variances requiring split-second decisions? Or, perhaps the spiritual life could be compared to a gymnast seeking to perform on a balance while coping with periodic, unexpected gusts of wind. The art of balance becomes precarious! My point is simply that when it comes to the spiritual life, of a consistent walk with God in Christ, it is not as simple as I was taught it would be.

This brings me to the question that is the inspiration for writing this book. How do you walk with God? Is there a secret or secrets? How are we to explain the inconsistencies in our walk after having become convinced of the great love of God for us revealed in and through Jesus Christ? Should the ongoing reality of struggle lead us to despair? When it comes to walking in obedience, is it just too complicated? Is that the only realistic conclusion? Is there no victory in Jesus until we stand complete in His presence?

Section 1

Preliminaries

The purpose of the chapters that follow is to introduce the spiritual life with a general overview, believing that learning is facilitated when the 'forest' is first conceptualized before proceeding to the 'trees', the particulars, the constituent parts. It is when the whole is perceived that the component parts are more readily understood.

It will be argued that walking with God is not an easy endeavor in that it requires knowledge and diligence. Unfortunately, we often think that the struggle with sin can be resolved by rigidly adopting a formula that we have learned from others we respect, but in reality, our walk with God is a personal journey. Yet there are universal principles that are indispensable. It seems that we have all learned retrospectively that perceptions of progress and folly are sometimes twins. The assurance that we are in the family comes from knowing that a struggle is present between what we know we should be and a reoccurring inconsistency of accomplishment. The normal Christian life is one ordered in such a manner to reflect increasingly the character of God. The fact of struggle is proof that we are in the family of God because we have experienced a radically renovating experience that has brought to us new perspectives, priorities, and passions.

1

PRELIMINARIES AND PREVIEW

THE PLACE TO BEGIN: THE BROADEST PERSPECTIVE

As we approach a discussion of the spiritual life, the daily walk as gospel people, perhaps the place to begin is to reflect on the external reasons for our struggles. Why is it that we all have areas of success, areas wherein we enact the application of the gospel to our immediate situation and generally make the right decisions reflecting integrity of character? On the other hand, why do we all struggle with what has been called 'the secret lusts of the heart'? Why do we shade the expression of truth by negligence and distortion, so that we appear wiser than we actually are at times? Why do we become overwhelmed with anxieties and fears of what could be, or how things will turn out, when deep down in our hearts we know that God is altogether omnipotent, sovereign, and fiercely committed to us? Why do we allow past miscues to rob us of peace, while Christ is so real to us in many ways? Simply put, why don't our struggles go away?

I think there are several general reasons for this, and I would like to investigate them with you.

The Technique Management Myth

First, when we listen to our trusted authorities, they often give the impression that, if we will only adopt the right technique, we will gain mastery over our sins. All we must do is 'do it the right way'. The difficulty with this assumption is that it is far too simplistic.

The attraction to specific techniques is more a child of Enlightenment rationalism than a reflection of the Holy Scriptures. Has the church adopted the prevailing intellectual lens of our culture to reduce complex issues to a linear method of sequence that, we are told, will lead to success? That is, the distinct formulation of goals leading to definable methods and the pursuit of definite steps, a process, will inevitably bring us to the realization of our goals. It is simply the matter of doing it the right way.

It would seem to me that the assumption of an easily achieved, simplistic, and formulaic approach to walking with God might be designated by some as effective communication, but it can leave the struggling saint in a disheartening dizziness of depression and disappointment, maybe leading to apathy. The problem with this approach is that the spiritual life loses its mystical dynamic and becomes a quest for conformity to rules, sequences, and regulations.

The Reality Personality Cults

Second, in listening to pastors and in reading a variety of books, an error is made when our authority sources root their model of the spiritual life on their own personalities and experience. It appears easier to explain to people how you have overcome a particular solicitation than to help them understand how you struggle with the sins that you have not marginalized to a less than dominating place in your life. We are willing to share our experience, which may indeed be helpful, but not to alert people to the fact that we all have areas in which there is a lack of success.

The damage done by a lack of qualifying disclosure is that the impression is often taken that the person before us is living on a higher spiritual plane than we are, to admit that others are doing better than we are, and that in some areas we simply cannot succeed to rise above some imperfection of character or act. When we exude too much optimism, it can be discouraging to others in their walk with the Lord, and we may well delude ourselves when we give the impression that we have our spiritual act together, when we do not.

THE PENDANT FOR INSTANT SPIRITUALITY

Westerners do not like the thought that things cannot be accomplished quickly and understood simply. In football and baseball, at the professional and collegiate levels, we have instant replay when a call is questionable; in our kitchens, we have instant mashed potatoes and a variety of instant concoctions from ready-made meals to coffee, and, of course, there is the ever-present microwave oven. We prefer elevators and electric walkways at airports and apartment units because we seem to be in a constant hurry to reach our goals with the least expenditure of time as well as effort.

It may be a truism, at least it is argued by those who observe our hectic pace, that we are a driven people, intolerant of delays and impediments to swift progress in our accomplishments. Apparently, Christianity has not diminished this cultural trait for most of us and that is clearly true when it comes to harnessing a walk with God. The old prayer is true of us, if not humorous, 'Lord, teach me patience, and do it now!'

However, what if the state of regeneration by the Spirit is not the same as the state of our final redemption? What if growing in spiritual maturity is a lifelong process, an enduring struggle, with wonderful victories at times, but simultaneously the discovery of new darkness in our souls, often in areas brought on by new circumstances, and that we are too-often infantile and underdeveloped in our reactions, deportment, and trust?

My argument is that spiritual growth is a matter of time, that none of us mature to the same degree or at the same pace in the same areas as other believers. The most salient point is that none of us reaches a state wherein the struggle with sin is behind us. In fact, as we grow older, we discover areas of immaturity heretofore unrealized as the challenges of our lives change.

For the idealist, the path of Christian growth may be disillusioning; for the realist, it is something to reckon with daily. I think our theories of progress should be tempered with Paul's personal insight: 'I find then the principle that evil is present with me, the one who wishes to do good .... Wretched man that I am! Who will set me free from the body of death ...? Thanks be to God through Jesus Christ our Lord ...' (Rom. 7:21, 24-25). The question before us is this: How can we struggle *successfully* so as to express more honorably our delight and appreciation of all that God has done for us?

A TRUTH TO GRASP: IT IS NOT THE THEORY, IT IS ABOUT GOD
It seems to me that the models that have repeatedly been presented by well-meaning teachers often do not work. Why? Is it that they do not offer sound advice and counsel? They frequently do! In fact, quite conflicting theories of walking with God actually work, although each has potential deficits. A different question to consider at this point is this: Why do we find very mature Christians in most of the varying expressions of sanctification theory?

For example, in many non-charismatic, evangelical churches, the theory often taught to parishioners emerged out of the Holiness Tradition that arose in England with the Keswick conferences and then became popular throughout the English-speaking world in the Bible Conference movement and Bible Institute movement towards the end of the nineteenth and into the twentieth century. People were taught that a Christian must have *two* life-changing, once-for-all experiences with God.

The first, of course, is redemption and the second has been called by various terms such as dedication, the filling of the Spirit, (rarely) eradication, or baptism with the Spirit. The point I am making is that the path to maturity, as it is often taught, is dependent on a second experience and requires a constancy of mental frame or trust that the experience is ongoing. After such a second experience, except for the eradicationists,[1] the struggle with sin supposedly lessens and victory becomes a distinct, though qualified, possibility. Thus, in this orientation to spiritual growth, the Romans 7 depiction by Paul is the *abnormal* Christian life.

Within the broad Reformed Tradition, the explanation of the path to spiritual maturity is different. In essence, regeneration, while distinguishable from sanctification, is not separated from it; it is not an option, dependent on voluntarism, because participation is required. There is a great moment when the Spirit of God awakens sinners, the fullness of the Spirit being instantaneously granted, though the experience of the Spirit as working out the character of Jesus is a progressive one. The final accomplishment of redemption awaits future glorification,

---

1. Eradicationists suggest that believers can be delivered completely in this life from the struggle with sin. It is a form of psychological visioning and redefinition of terms, such as the meaning of sin.

while the process of growing in Christlikeness is gradual, sometimes (often!) in baby-steps. What I have found is that when differing models both fail and succeed, it cannot be that the particular method is the key ingredient, because success is found in the common ingredients within the various explanations.

A variant of the broadly evangelical approach to the spiritual life is the Pentecostal understanding that a productive, obedient conformity to the will of God in thought and conduct is found in two primary spiritual experiences. The approach is distinct from non-Pentecostal Evangelicals in that the second step is designated as a second spiritual baptism, not *in* the Spirit but *with* the Spirit, manifested by the spiritual gift of speaking in tongues, following the pattern of Acts 2 or 1 Corinthians 11. An alteration of this approach can be found in the broader charismatic movements which do not mandate a particular spiritual gift as baptism-in-the-Spirit evidence. In each of the multi-step methods, the net result is empowerment.

Unless we are living in some kind of fantasy, the failures and discrepancies found in all of us between God's declarations and our behavior are facts. We all have the problem of dealing with imperfections. One of the goals in writing this book is to present viable principles of how to walk with God without overstating the acquisition of benefits or promising too little, or in either case being unfaithful to the text of the Bible.

SOME UNIVERSAL FUNDAMENTAL PRINCIPLES AS WE BEGIN
Before we launch into specifics, moving away from generalities, I would like us to think about some preliminary assumptions, some bedrock truths, that we must keep in mind when approaching the task of spiritual

development. The comments below are broad in nature, but they are integral to framing the discussion.

It seems that first, and foremost, the spiritual life is one of mental struggling. What one allows themselves to meditate upon, to dwell upon, becomes their values, and their values are revealed in conduct. Simply put, the old adage is indeed a truism. 'Input determines output; garbage in is garbage out.' What we fill our minds with – what consumes our mental energy – determines the course of our lives. Therefore, the most fundamental principle of the spiritual life, a life directed toward obedience to God, comes down to a triumvirate of 'knows': you must 'know your God'; you must 'know yourself'; you must 'know your circumstances'.

If our goal is to live in such a manner that conforms to the character of God – to the object of our delight and affection, we must know Him. If we are ignorant of the ways and values of the One we seek to please, we will find ourselves stumbling about in allegorical darkness to please Him. This point is what we might call 'the importance of the mental'. At a very basic realm of interpersonal communication, how can we appropriately communicate and have a wholesome relationship with a person we do not know – whether it be a parent, mate, child, or friend? It requires learning. It also is true of walking with the Lord. This means that we must get to know Him as the singularly supreme source of the knowledge of Himself, not merely about Him (what we might call secondary experience), but Him. We must become acquainted with the Bible because in it God has supremely revealed Himself.

However, there is more about walking with the Lord than merely becoming a student of the Bible; we must become students of ourselves. We are all different! Simply put, 'One size does not fit all.' Instructions for another person may not be helpful to us because it does not connect with our constitutional makeup, our degree of spiritual growth at any given point, or the uniqueness of our spiritual struggles.

We are all different in many ways. At various stages of spiritual growth, we may not have the discipline to address successfully areas of need in our lives. Perhaps, it is weariness from overwork, simply trying too hard to accomplish more than we should, resulting in a lack of sleep, grumpiness, or sheer insensitivity. An underlying principle, it seems to me, is that we must become aware of how we are internally wired!

Furthermore, we must learn that solicitations to sin come in different forms and in various circumstances for all of us. We all should be students of how we internally respond to external stimulus. What may be an occasion for slippage for one may not be for another! The devil is a master strategist and psychologist; he knows how to probe into our weaknesses and gullibilities, striking at the most opportune moment. He can manipulate our weaknesses, taking advantage of our undeveloped characters. To avoid needless spiritual decline, we must become aware of how the devil, and his numerous minions, get us off track, and then we must use that knowledge to become aware of danger when such becomes apparent.

Are you one that takes on more obligations than you can manage? Do you need a certain amount of rest to maintain a modicum of stability? Does the company of certain people tend to pull you downward, or lead you into temptations you would not otherwise consider? Do you have a short emotional fuse, and have you figured out the triggers that ignite it? We must all learn how it is that we 'enter into temptation.'

One of Luther's clever insights was this: 'You cannot prevent the birds from flying over your head, but you can prevent them from making a nest in your hair.' His point, it seems to me, was that we should be aware of 'the birds', knowing enough about them to deal with them at their first approach.

DISCUSSION QUESTIONS

1. How would you say that your initial experience of the Lord's redemptive grace differs from your experience now? Was there some lapse of time before you understood the moral implications of Christ in your life?

2. Have you found that some spiritual life teachers seem to understand that it is easier to walk in obedience to Christ than you have experienced? Why do you think this has been the case?

3. If walking with God is both art and science, why do you think we have placed more emphasis on the science of it, methodology, than the realization that we have come to Christ as individuals, each uniquely shaped by Him?

4. What is the possible danger of following the example and instruction of others when you and I have been crafted uniquely by God to see what others do not see and thus serve Him in ways others cannot envision?

5. Is there a positive side to the fact that we do not all struggle with the same deficiencies of character? Could it be that a positive is that each of us can help each

other because there are areas in our walk where we have struggled successfully? Are there not areas where God has given you practical, helpful insight to help others? What might be one or two of them?

6. As this study commences, what kind of help are you seeking? What struggles in your personal life do you seek to overcome?

2

IMPORTANT INGREDIENTS IN WALKING WITH GOD:

AN OVERVIEW

In a very real sense, the first two chapters of this book are broad in nature, canvassing general issues as one begins to think through the meaning of the spiritual life. Before moving away from those generalities, I will make a few additional comments and refer to some bedrock truths that we must keep in mind when approaching the task of spiritual development. Perhaps a way to summarize the points that I am trying to make is this:

First, walking with God involves intimacy with the Bible, an acquaintance with the great book beyond the merely intellectual, content level. It requires an affectionate attraction that is reflected, not only in reading its pages, but by a preoccupation with it in our thought-life, our involuntary meditations.

Second, walking with God involves the realization that it is not a matter of mastering a particular technique or a specific routine. It is far more than a prescribed rhythm of activities; rather it is about the institution of habits that become almost second nature to us.

Third, walking with God involves the harsh reality of coming to grips with our weaknesses. The blunt truth is that coming to know God, as He is revealed to us through

Christ, does not incline us to some plateau of victory over sin in every facet of our being, certainly not in our thought-life. Though we have entered into the triumph of the great second Adam, the sinful nature that we inherited through the first Adam does not go away. Our entrance through Christ and the regenerating mercies of the Holy Spirit do give us new perspectives and new priorities, but they do not cure our identity with old Adam in our behavioral patterns. Redemption does not renovate our natures; only death will put an end to our struggles with regrettable attitudes and actions.

Fourth, walking with God involves the recognition that the spiritual life is a process. The endeavor to walk after the Redeemer who redeemed us is a journey. While there may be great moments of insight and significant turning points in our walk with God, there are no quick fixes. It is a task that requires resolve, steadfastness, and courage. It demands such a degree of holding Christ as our highest priority that no degree of failure or disappointment causes us to capitulate for lesser goals. I have been captured by a resolution Jonathan Edwards wrote as one of his life goals on 8 July 1723: 'Never to give over, nor in the least to slacken, my fight against my corruptions no matter how unsuccessful I may be' (#56).

The Realization that God is at Work in us

Walking with God means, as a fundamental starting-point and basic assumption, coming to grips with the utter goodness of God, the splendor and congruity of all His attributes, and His unquestioned prerogative to govern, direct, and shape our lives. This is what we might call 'the ever-present reality'. Simply put, 'For we are His workmanship, created in Christ Jesus for good works which God prepared beforehand that we would walk in them' (Eph. 2:10). It begins with the realization that we were made for Him, not He for us. He does not function in our lives as some sort of cosmic Santa Claus, singularly devoted to maximizing our interests and delights. The purpose of our lives is to reflect His character, and it is through doing so that we glorify God (but more about that subsequently).

While God has revealed Himself truly to His people, He has not revealed Himself to us exhaustively. There are reasons for happenings in our lives that are beyond our grasping, even with a modicum of insight. It seems that not one of us would have written our life stories in the way that they have unfolded, but what we know is that the One who orchestrates the stage upon which our lives are played out is trustworthy, kind beyond all measure, and generous without limit. He is the One who does more than we can ask or even think. This affirmed, it does not mean that His goodness comes wrapped in a blanket of comfort and exuberant delight, but rather it comes often with pain. The manner of His shaping us is sometimes negative from our perspective. God uses pain, weakness, tragedy, and failures to mature us in our walk with God.

Have you not uttered words or thoughts similar to Gideon's when he responded to God under the perilous threat of the Midianites? 'Oh my lord, if the Lord is with us, why then did these things happen to us?' (Judg. 6:13). The words of Job echo in our ears in the midst of our disappointments and pain: 'For what I fear comes upon me, and what I dread befalls me. I am not at ease, nor am I quiet, and not at rest, but turmoil comes' (Job 3:25-26). It is only retrospectively that any of us will say what Joseph said to his brothers in Genesis 50:20: 'You meant evil against me, *but* God meant it for good.' While other texts can be assembled in this regard, the point is that growing in the grace of Christ is not always pleasant. The shaping and fine tuning of our lives to reflect the character of God involves disappointment and pain at times.

Furthermore, while there are many things that we will never understand in our life-experience, it is fundamentally important to live in the reality that randomness does not exist in this world, that God is wonderfully sovereign, that nothing can happen in our lives that He has not permitted for a positive purpose. The depth of our comfort is not found in the limit of our ability to grasp and understand what is happening, but in the character and trustworthiness of the God we trust. The path toward our eternal home may be strewn with boulders, seemingly covered by landslides, that cause inexplicable detours, but the path is all absolutely sure because sustained by the oft-invisible hand of divine providence. We have a sure end because of the character of our sure hope, the Lord Jesus Christ.

I find myself enamored by the insight and wisdom found in the first question proposed in the great Heidelberg Catechism (1562), enamored, in part, that it is placed first. The way to walk with God is to settle once and for all, though we all need constant reminders, that God has each of us in the shadow of His protective mercies, guidance, and grace, no matter what befalls!

Q. What is your only comfort in life and in death?
A. That I am not my own, but belong – body and soul, in life and in death – to my faithful Savior, Jesus Christ. He has fully paid for all my sins with his precious blood and has set me free from the tyranny of the devil. He also watches over me in such a way that not a hair can fall from my head without the will of my Father in heaven; in fact, all things must work together for

my salvation. Because I belong to him, Christ, by his Holy Spirit, assures me of eternal life and makes me wholeheartedly willing and ready from now on to live for him.

Finally, we must understand, as we begin the discussion of walking with God, that His primary intent for us is the development of our character, and not personal success in the realms of health, family, or professional careers. Such values are important and are honoring to God, certainly important to us; but God's goal for each of us is godliness in every and all circumstances. While we desire to experience divine significance in and through our lives, shedding forth His worth for all to see, it may very well be that we may not have the same view of how we are to be significant as God might. God may have a different course for us than personal prosperity and cultural success. Simply put, God is more interested in your being, your character, than in your doing; how we conduct our lives, the choices we make, is the way we reflect His character. However, the two are distinct, and duty must flow from character!

THE AWARENESS THAT WE ARE THE PROBLEM

Walking with God is not an easy endeavor because we are often the problem. An old saying captures the point, 'We have met the enemy and he is us.' Or as the saying goes, 'We are our own worst enemies.' This is what we might call 'the ever-present fact of sin.' The portrait that the Bible paints of the saints of God enshrined in humanity is not beautiful at times; the record of the people of God revealed in the Bible is telling. We all possess a blindness of mind and soul, a selfish will that gives at times sinful expression, and an independent streak that is reluctant to trust that the ways of the Lord are pure and right. While the benefits are many, and growth in the things of God is our promise from Him by the Spirit, the Christ walk is a struggle.

I am arguing that sin is an ever-present reality for all believers. It is interesting to me that our brokenness becomes increasingly more evident as we seek to engage in the daily walk. You and I will never have a motive as pure as the character of God, unsullied and apart from self-interest, until we enter into the presence of God. It is true that we are now in Christ, that we are clothed impeccably with His righteousness from the perspective of the great divine judge before whom we have been acquitted by Christ; however, what I just described is our standing before God, not our present state before Him. The load of sin on Pilgrim's back in John Bunyan's epic fell off when he encountered the cross, yet his final release for tormenting solicitations, such as doubt and missteps, awaited his assured entrance into the distant city, and it will not for us until we enter the 'distant city'.

A Caution as we Start

While the aforesaid may seem to drape a cold blanket over our enthusiasm, our encouragement, to walk with the Lord, and while you might be thinking that I am a little on the pessimistic side, let me assure you that I am not. What should be our focus as we seek to walk with God, to enjoy the breath of His presence, and to reflect His glory? Is the spiritual life one of drudgery, plodding along with our heads down and wincing in pain? Is the best of the Christian walk what Henry Ford described about life from his perspective? 'Plodding from one failure to the next without a loss of enthusiasm.'

My answer is a resounding No! No! No! Why is it not so, given the constant struggles that we all have? The answer is found in the object of our affection, the person in whom we have come to have great delight, the Lord Jesus Christ. The wonder of His incarnate life and sacrificial death for us, evidenced by His resurrection, is utterly overwhelming to our senses. The primary motivation for each of us is to conform to Him out of profound and unrelenting appreciation for all that He has done for us. This is what we might call 'the wonder of redemption.'

What for many is the ignominious end of a pathetically misunderstood and deluded maniac is for us the greatest moment of all of human history. For us, the event of Calvary, followed by the resurrection of Jesus, is proof positive that the man from Galilee is the 'name above all names,' the Son of God and the Son of Man. In experiencing the life of God, as mediated through the Spirit witnessing to the wonder of His accomplishments for us, He has become the delightful meditation and preoccupation that causes us to want to know Him better. You and I have come to life; you and I have come to understand the meaning of life; you and I have become a people filled with hope because of Calvary. When delight and desire motivate a task, the endeavor becomes easier to bear. The Christian walk is about the reconstruction of our priorities and goals in light of the cross of Christ.

As I close this chapter, I want to gather some of the threads of our discussion to this point. First, the Christian life is a mental struggle. The gateway to the affections is the mind; it is your likes and dislikes that formulate your choices and your choices are a result of information available to you. What you entertain, what you think about, what you focus upon, is what you will chose, do, and become. Therefore, right thoughts are of utmost importance; good information is important for decision making.

Second, the spiritual life boils down to actions based on priorities. The internal manifests itself in the external. Hence, the development of internal habits is crucial to proper performance (within our topic area, that is to have increasingly greater degrees of conformity to Christ).

Third, walking with God is a process; we are all on a journey. There is no beatific plateau in this life. We all have great moments, but life is exceedingly complex.

Fourth, it is confusing to realize that there are godly people believing very diverse things about how to walk with God. If diversity of methods obtains the same hopeful ends, this would suggest that a key ingredient is not any particular method. All methods entail 'trust and obey.' The question before us is, how can we come to a willingness to 'trust and obey'?

DISCUSSION QUESTIONS

1. What cautions, and qualifications, have you learned as you broach a meaningful approach to enriching your walk with God?

2. What are you consciously doing to access good and wholesome thoughts? What can you do?

3. Why do you think it is easier to do than to be, doing good and appropriate things while neglecting to address the defects of our character?

4. Discouragement through a lack of success is often a perennial problem for many believers. How has this chapter helped you in your struggles with failure?

5. When we are faced with limited knowledge, are we at the end of the possibility of comfort? Is help in life primarily an information question or is it a focus question?

Section 2

The Actions and Provisions of God to Promote Spiritual Growth

In this set of chapters, the spiritual life is considered from the divine perspective. It seeks to answer the question of the divine enablement which ensures that our walk with God will not be a dismal struggle, but a wonderful journey of increasing delight and conformity in our pursuit of the will of God, the One who alone has brought us into a community where love, harmony, and delight are unstintingly ours to embrace and enjoy.

The provision of the Lord for His children can be described as having two components: first, there are spiritual advantages that He has planted within our very beings, assuring us that our struggles with the remnants of sin's once universal reign will end in its complete annihilation with the subsequent eternal enjoyment of God, rejoicing in His presence and delighting in His character forever; and, second, the spiritual advantages that He brings to us through the shaping of external events and circumstances, both curtailing and enhancing our behavioral patterns.

3

The Most Fundamental Question:
Why do we exist?

At this point in our study of the spiritual life, I want to leave the introductory matters discussed in chapters one and two and plunge more deeply into the subject before us. In the next four chapters, I will address certain theological topics that are fundamental to conceptualizing the spiritual life. It may seem strange to begin our deeper study with the fundamental question of existence, yet sometimes simple questions provide profound insight. Why did the all-sufficient, self-existent God, who was not seeking to remediate any personal deficiencies, create all that we see around us? Can an answer to that question help us understand the spiritual life more clearly?

The Being of God
What words come to your mind when you think about God? What terms would you choose? It is most common, when answering such questions, to speak of the attributes of God; that is, the character of God revealed in His names and actions (what do they tell us about Him?). However, the question I am proposing is a more general one. Taking all the evidence in the Bible about the character of God, what few overarching descriptive words would you chose?

Maybe you would choose the noun *perfection*, an intrinsic quality, since God does all things in conformity with unsullied congruity to flawlessness, precision, exactness, and rightness. In fact, He is the definition of all those terms. A second term you might suggest is *beauty* because God's multi-faceted character, when seen as a whole, is the epitome of symmetry, plurality, and proportions, a workable general definition of beauty. Another term might be *love* as we reflect on the apostle's statement that 'God is love' (1 John 4:8), suggesting that all of His actions are a function of His character. In fact, it may be argued that love is the highest kind of beauty because it is never blighted in any way in the being of God.

THE PURPOSE OF THE DIVINE CREATION

This brings me to the point, given all that we know about God – His independence, self-existence, and complete self-satisfaction – for the reason of His creative action. Is there a clue in this to the meaning of the spiritual life? It is clear that God has no deficiencies that He wanted or needed to correct and so sought to resolve them by creative activity. We can also say that, since nothing existed outside of God before He created,[1] there was no external necessity for His creative activity. Thus, we can say that God's motive is rooted in His own internal desires.

The answer for why God created is found within His holy, self-determining self. It seems that it is rooted in the inter-trinitarian delight of God to manifest or reveal His own character. His motive for creation was to multiply the adoration and praise of Himself. God delights in the effusion, the emanation, of Himself and so created

---

1. '... by Him all things were created' (Col. 1:16); 'For from Him and through Him and to Him are all things' (Rom. 11:36).

an external manifestation of His character, a world of beauty, harmony, and love. 'Let all the earth fear the Lord; let all the inhabitants of the earth stand in awe of him' (Ps. 33:8). God rightly seeks His own glorification which is not an empty boast simply because He alone is altogether beautiful.

The Bible expresses the notion of God's self-glorification by the word *glory*. The term has two essential nuances in the Holy Scriptures. For example, glory is frequently used to express God's internal qualities, what theologians describe as attributes. When used as such, it has reference to His excellency, dignity, worthiness, greatness, or beauty (the perfect symmetry and balance of those qualities, and more). Yet another usage, pertinent to this discussion, is that glory often refers to the display or manifestation of those internal qualities. Ezekiel proclaims, 'And behold I saw the glory of the God of Israel coming from the way of the east. And the earth shone with His glory' (Ezek. 43:2). The phrases 'name of God' and 'glory of God' are often used interchangeably in the Bible. God says to Moses in Exodus 33:19: 'I Myself will make all My goodness to pass before you.' In Psalm 8:1, David exclaims: 'O LORD, our Lord, How majestic is Your name in all the earth, Who have displayed Your splendor above the heavens!'

The superb manifestation of divine glory was in the Lord Jesus Christ. 'No one has seen God at any time, the only begotten of God who is in the bosom of the Father, He has explained Him' (John 1:18). In our Lord's prayer before Gethsemane, He said, 'And now, Father, glorify Me together with Yourself, with the glory which I had with You before the world was. I have manifested Your name to the men whom You gave Me out of the world' (John 17:5-6). In John's grand description of the redeemed in heaven, he says that 'they will see His face, and His name shall be on their foreheads' (Rev. 22:4), meaning righteousness will describe them.

If God's own self-glorification is the ultimate cause of creation, then we can make the claim that the purpose of the divine creation is to glorify Him, to reflect His glory, His character, and only that. Who does not stand on the edge of the Grand Canyon, observing the vastness of the cleavage of the earth, the changing colors as the clouds pass by, and think of the divine Creator? Can you watch a majestic stallion trot so effortlessly and not think of Him? Sit on a beach beside a large body of water and observe the changing hues, the plethora of colors, as the sun sets, and who do you think of in the quietness of a meditative moment? The Psalmist said it for all of us: 'The heavens are telling the glory of God and their expanse is declaring the works of His hands; Day to day pours forth speech, and night to night reveals knowledge' (Ps. 19:1-2).

Paul states the case bluntly: 'Because that which is known about God is revealed to them for God made it evident to them. For since the creation of the world His invisible attributes, His power and divine nature, have been clearly seen, being understood through what has been made so that they are without excuse' (Rom. 1:19-20). God created the natural world so that it would reflect His beauty back upon Himself. The natural world was created to show forth the symmetry and beauty of God in a lower way than His image-bearers; He made us so that we might join all nature in a chorus of adulation and praise. William Henry Draper (1855–1933) composed the lyrics of an English Christian hymn often sung at Easter; the idea was gathered from a poem by St Francis of Assisi based on Psalm 148.

All creatures of our God and King,
Lift up your voice and with us sing,
O praise Him, Alleluia.
Thou burning sun with golden beam,
Thou silver moon with softer gleam,
O praise Him, O praise Him,
Alleluia, Alleluia, Alleluia.

Thou rushing wind that art so strong,
Ye clouds that sail in Heaven along,
O praise Him, Alleluia.
Thou rising moon in praise rejoice,
Ye lights of evening find a voice,
O praise Him, O praise Him,
Alleluia, Alleluia, Alleluia.

Let all things their Creator bless,
And worship Him in humbleness,
O praise Him, Alleluia.[2]

THE CREATION OF HUMANITY

If the divine purpose of the creation was to multiply and reflect God's greatness and beauty, and since the creation of mankind is His greatest and highest creative achievement, it is logical, and biblically accurate, to say that our creation was for the same reason. The prophet Isaiah, speaking for God, said: 'Everyone who is called by My name, and whom I created for My glory, whom I have formed, even whom I have made' (Isa. 43:7). Paul says it this way: '... from Him, and through Him, and to Him are all things. To God be the glory forever. Amen' (Rom. 11:36).

Men and women stand in a unique relationship to God and to each other, an intimacy unlike that sustained

2. This traditional Christian hymn has appeared in numerous hymn books beginning in the early twentieth century. I am quoting the lyrics from *Great Hymns of the Faith* (Grand Rapids: Zondervan Corporation, 1974), 31.

within nature. To understand why this is so, we turn to the creation account in Genesis 1. 'And God created man in His own image, in the image of God He created Him; male and female He created them' (Gen. 1:27). As scholars have noted, this verse indicates that mankind was not only created *in* the image of God, we were created *as* the image of God. Though much effort has gone into defining the exact nature of the image of God in us (rationality, creativity, rule, volition), what remains a consistent finding is that of relationality. While the capacity for relationship is not unique to human beings, the human capacity is unique. Human beings occupy a singular position in relationship to God. We were made by Him and share with Him the qualities of communal interaction at an intellectual level far deeper than any other of His earthly creatures.

Thus, the uniqueness of mankind is that we bear, in created form, the relational qualities of our triune Creator – the inter-trinitarian communication, rooted in filial affection and delight, a mutual bond of self-giving, and other-oriented perspectives. Solomon recognized this when saying, 'O Lord, the God of Israel, there is no God like You in heaven above or on earth beneath, keeping covenant and showing loving kindness to Your servants who walk before You with all their heart' (1 Kings 8:23). The apostle John said it this way: 'Beloved, let us love one another, for love is from God; and everyone who loves is born of God and knows God' (1 John 4:7).

It is by being created in the image of God that the purpose of our creation is discovered. As unique in all of God's creation, men and women have the capacity to show forth the invisible character of God through social relationships (marriage, friends, co-workers, church). Imagine that! Humans can reflect the character of God!

When God sees Himself in us, He is glorified because He simply sees Himself! I am reminded of a poem that has found its way into many of our hymnals, written by Thomas O. Chisholm (1866–1960) in the late nineteenth century. It is entitled 'Oh To Be Like Thee.' God has stamped His image on all of us; we are like Him!

> Oh! to be like Thee, full of compassion,
> Loving, forgiving, tender and kind,
> Helping the helpless, cheering the fainting,
> Seeking the wand'ring sinner to find.
>
> Oh! to be like Thee, lowly in spirit,
> Holy and harmless, patient and brave;
> Meekly enduring cruel reproaches,
> Willing to suffer, others to save.
>
> Refrain:
> *Oh! to be like Thee, oh! to be like Thee,*
> *Blessed Redeemer, pure as Thou art;*
> *Come in Thy sweetness, come in Thy fullness;*
> *Stamp Thine own image deep on my heart.*[3]

THE FRACTURING OF THE DIVINE INTENT

The writer to the Hebrews makes us aware that though mankind, as well as all things, was created as a visible extension of the beauty of God, such is not now the case. After quoting Psalm 8:6, 'You make him to rule over the works of Your hands ... You have put all things under his feet,' he alludes to a sobering reality ('But now we do not see all things subjected to him' [Heb. 2:8b]). The failure of Adam to act in obedience to God culminated in a tragedy of cosmic proportions. We now find ourselves in

---

3. I am quoting the lyrics from *Great Hymns of the Faith* (Grand Rapids: Zondervan Corporation, 1974), 316.

a world that has become disfigured, the ground is cursed (Gen. 3:17), thorns and weeds dot the landscape of our gardens! We read in Romans 8:19-23 that the creation itself is groaning, awaiting its redemption. Silver tarnishes, the earth cracks from a lack of moisture, flowers wilt, and leaves fall from our trees! Something happened!

Adam's rebellion not only blighted the ability of natural creation to mirror the character of God; it has brought into the human realm grave changes from the divine intent. Created to be like Him, displaying social harmony and care, the cries on our streets, the tears in our homes, the horrid trivialization of the value of human life, and the clash of nations, tells all of us that something went astray. Simply look around and you will see what I mean! Instead of the fruit of the Spirit (Gal. 5:22-23), the character of God Himself, mankind mirrors the fruit of the flesh (Gal. 5:19-21). Simply to name a few of the fifteen characteristics of mankind in a fallen world makes the point that social harmony has been dissolved (enmities, strife, jealousy, outbursts of anger, disputes, dissensions, factions, envy). Mankind, having been created to mirror the character of God, presents at best a distorted, disfigured, truncated image of God. God made us for the supreme purpose of showing forth His glory, but that ability has been diluted, if not lost. Can anyone see the face of God when couples, covenanting to live in harmony, manifest disharmony in the midst of broken promises? Can anyone in the workplace reveal the character of God when the integrity of a day's wage for a day's work is invested in self-centred preoccupations? Promises, promises, we live in a world of broken promises!

A Story Unfolding: Mankind Restored

Though I have painted a less than flattering picture of humanity at large, and you may find yourself a little confused, let me bring this discussion into the realm of the spiritual life. What is the spiritual life that subsequently I will attempt to describe? Simply put, it is about how we as fallen, often selfish, people can remove the tarnish that has collected on the mirrors of our lives so that we can reflect more wonderfully the beauty of God. We were created to reveal to a visible world the harmony and beauty of the invisible God, and that is the topic of this book. How do we, as struggling believers, polish the mirror and remove some of the tarnish that prevents an accurate reflection to others of the God we love and serve?

Adam's rebellion seemed to put an end to the desire of God to use His image-bearers to reflect His character so that all the world could see Him. Satan looked as though he had throttled God's purpose of self-glorification through creation. But such is not the case. God is restoring humanity, you and me, to reflect His invisible glory! While the final restoration awaits 'the new heavens and the new earth,' God is triumphing today, people are seeing Him through us. How is God doing it? That is the story before us.

DISCUSSION QUESTIONS

1. Can you and I grow spiritually, reflecting the character of God, in isolation from interpersonal relationships? If we are in the image of God, and God is the very definition of community in the Godhead, can we grow without intimate relationships?

2. Why is it not vanity that God would seek His praise, that He would seek to be known? Why then is it vain for us to seek personal recognition and praise?

3. Because God's purpose in all of creation is to seek His glory reflected back upon Him in praise, does it not take away God's freedom since He created out of necessity? Since He had to do it, in what sense can we say that God is free and not free? How do we understand 'had' in relationship to God?

4. In what ways do you think the character of God is most reflected by your life and lifestyle? In what ways do you think the mirror of your life is tarnished and needs polishing to improve reflective capacities?

5. You and I know that what God ordains for creation cannot be prevented. God is making mirrors and you are one of them. In your work how do you think you could shine better? In your marriage, home life with the rearing of children, in your dating if single, with aging parents, or in the turmoil of securing a solid professional education to fulfill your life goals, are there ways you can improve? Rest assured in this endeavor that God's purpose for you to be an unblemished mirror for eternity will come to fruition in the restoration of all things!

4

The Meaning of the Redemption Experience:

What does it accomplish in a broken world in the lives of broken people?

In the previous chapter, we explored the purposes of God for creation, suggesting that God's primary intent, though there are many consequential ramifications, is to multiply the extension of His beauty with the result that He is glorified by beholding Himself, His very own character, in His creation. The God of heaven is triune (Father, Son, and Holy Spirit) and the love between them is shared in equal proportion. God is a relational, communal being. Love, by its very nature, seeks expression and multiplication. All of creation was intended by God to reflect His glory, so that in beholding His own character, as in a mirror, He would be delighted (who would not like to admire beauty?). The introduction of sin into our world has simply tarnished the 'silver in our reflective mirrors,' a blight-causing dysfunctionalism, so an abortion of ends has resulted. It is not hard to find evidence of this in all of our social relationships, whether it be in our homes, marketplaces, or churches. Instead of reflecting the character, beauty, and love of God, too often our lives have become snarled in complexity, grudges, and hostility (often, but not always, based on frustrated dreams, unspeakable disappointments, and painful hurts).

The purpose before us in this chapter is to begin an investigation of what God has done, and is currently doing, to reverse the effects of the Fall. In this and two subsequent chapters, the focus will be on the actions of God. What is God doing to bring a greater reflective shine to our mirrors? The one word that might most accurately describe the actions of God is *redemption*. God is calling out a people and is delivering them from the curse of sin and death by increasing their capacity to effuse and emanate His glories.

What is the Message of the Bible?

A way to discover the message of a book is to read the last chapter. Authors commonly conclude their work by summarizing the focal point of what they sought to argue. While the Bible may not exactly fit the pattern of literary formatting in our day, the final chapters tell us something very important relative to the purposes of God; something fundamental to understand what the spiritual life is about ultimately. The story line of the Bible can be summarized this way: creation accomplished, creation marred, and creation restored. The divine restoration of the blighted creation is taking place today in the divine calling of men and women, boys and girls, to Himself. The restoration process will become a finalized reality in heaven when all who have responded to His message, which was delivered to us by Christ and proclaimed by the apostles, are gathered to be with Him forever, beholding His beauty and adoring Him with endless praise and recognition. God is today reversing the effects of the Fall by calling a people to be His children, to be with Him eternally.

The Bible begins with the creation of a habitat for humanity, a garden (Gen. 1–2), with God dwelling among His creation; it will end with an eternal celestial city in the new heavens and the new earth (Rev 21–22), with God in the midst of it all, not with a couple who would spurn His goodness and doubt His integrity and His trustworthiness, but with myriads from all the nations, when all His promises will be fulfilled toward us. Will we not even be ashamed that we did not trust Him more in this life? Let me explain:

The Creation	The Recreation
Light without Luminaries (1:3) (21:23)	Light without Luminaries
(God's glory dimmed now [Gen 3–Rev 20])	
No curses (1:31)	No curses (21:4, 22:3)
(The earth cursed, and the couple broken [Gen 3–Rev 20])	
A river flowing outward (2:8)	A river flowing outward (22:1)
(River is symbolic of life and prosperity, only death and turmoil now flow forth [Gen 3–Rev 20])	
A tree of life (2:9)	A tree of Life (22:14,19)
(Tree is symbolic of spiritual life, now lost [Gen 3–Rev 20])	
God with His people (3:8)	God with His people (21:3)
Unrighteous excluded (3:24)	Unrighteous excluded (22:11)

The Bible envisions three eras of history; scholars commonly speak of the Old Testament era, the New Testament era, and the Kingdom; or, a period that was, a period that is, and a period that will be. Hebrews 1:1 speaks of a time long ago when God spoke 'to the fathers in the prophets' ('the times of ignorance,' Acts 17:30). He has also spoken 'in these last days.' There the writer is indicating that the Jews thought of only two ages – former times and latter times. They thought they were living in the former times, because they did not think the 'latter times' had come in the spiritualized kingdom inaugurated by Jesus

Christ. The 'latter times' are divided into two parts – the time between Christ's two advents and a period of His full, perfect reign after His second coming. Hebrews 9:10 refers to the last phase of the 'last days' as the 'time of the reformation' or 'consummation of the ages' (Heb. 9:26). Peter, in his sermon recorded by Luke (Acts 3:19-24), says that the prophets from Samuel announced 'these days,' the latter days, and that Jesus will not return to earth 'until the period of the restoration of all things' (v. 21), or the latter part of the latter days.

GOD AND THE GATHERING OF A NEW PEOPLE

From a biblical perspective, we can say that God is gathering a people to enjoy His presence, to delight in His beauty with adoring praise. He is creating a coterie of folks; He is constantly reversing the effects of the Fall. Our God is a relational being; He delights in the reality of the multiplication of His glory. While creation groans and suffers under the weight of the curse (Rom. 8:22), God is calling a people out of the kingdom of darkness and translating them into the yet-to-be-completed kingdom of His Son (Col. 1:13).

The Bible is the story of the restoration of a dwelling place where God can once more live among His people; hence, though secondarily, the Bible is the story of the defeat of God's arch-rival Satan and the fulfillment of His intentions to create a world wherein He alone receives praise. How is God doing this? What one word can we employ to describe it? The one word is *redemption*. God through Christ, by means of the Spirit, is gathering a people who will one day collectively, and in holiness of character, dwell in God's presence fulfilling the purpose of their creation. The question immediately before us is this: How is God currently redeeming us so that our mirrors reflect His glory today, and so that in a future day we will never need to be re-polished through repentance, with a change of attitude and demeanor?

THE ESSENCE OF THE EXPERIENCE OF REDEMPTION

The goal before us now is to describe the nature of the redemptive experience. What most deeply changes when God enters a life, granting an understanding of Jesus' claims and forgiveness through Him? How can the redemptive experience be described? Simply put, it is the infusion of the life of God into the depths of our very being. However, we can be more specific.

First, we can truly say that the redemptive experience is a work of God because an effect partakes in the nature of its cause. If you want to have a flowerbed of marigolds to decorate your landscape, you do not plant cucumber seed and reasonably hope for yellow, golden, bronze marigolds. You, obviously, plant marigold seeds because what you want (the effect) is marigolds. If salvation is the gift of life without end, eternal life, its source must be eternal. Peter, for example, speaks of Christians as 'partakers of the divine nature' (2 Pet. 1:4). I am my father's son, good and not so good, because I am my father's son!

Second, since God is spirit (John 4:24), meaning immaterial, He is without observable characteristics (volume, shape, or proportion). 'No one has seen God at any time...' (John 1:18). Hence, we know God as a result of His works; His works tell us who He is and what He is like, His actions revealing His character. The ancients observed the actions of God and named Him accordingly. For example, when God provided a water-source to save Ishmael and Hagar from dehydration in the wilderness, Hagar provided for us a descriptive name of God (Gen. 16:13), 'the one who sees' our need

(El Roi). When Isaac came with his father to Mount Moriah to make a sacrifice, he recognized that they had the elements necessary for a sacrifice but no animal. Abraham told his son that God would provide for them (Gen. 22:13-14), so we have 'Jehovah Jireh,' meaning 'the God who provides.' His works are consistent with His character, the two being distinguishable, but inseparable. Since salvation is a gift from God to us, and since the gift partakes of the character of the Giver, salvation must be otherworldly, an intrusion into this realm. It is divine life in our souls. In so providing, God has made it possible for us to reflect His character, having placed His life, His character, in us (God is gloried when He sees Himself).

THE DIVINE EXISTENCE OF GOD WITHIN US

Scholars have found it difficult to describe the essence of the life of God in the believer. How do you define the presence of God within us? Some have called the divine life a 'new principle' that brings about in us new priorities and values. The Bible speaks of being 'spiritually minded,' suggesting a set of new directives. Perhaps we can describe it with words like 'a spiritual sense of things,' 'a relish or delight in divine things,' 'a new disposition,' 'a sense of divine excellency,' or 'a taste of heaven.' Salvation, I think, is the personal experience of the glory of God in Jesus Christ; it is the implantation of the infinite, the very life of God, in finite creatures. Since the divine life within us is the infused life of God, and God in His very character is holy love (1 John 4:7-10), this new abiding principle, partaking of its source, is revealed in the form of love ('We love because Christ loved us ...' (1 John 4:19-21). 'God so loved the world that He gave His only begotten Son ...' (John 3:16). It was the inter-trinitarian love of God, mutually and constantly expressed in the members of the Godhead, that sought multiplication and resulted in effusion, the extension of love's display.

THE AFFECTIONS AND SALVATION

The point of this section is to raise a question that, though it may seem unimportant to the discussion of the spiritual life, is in reality crucial. Perhaps we can ask the question this way: In what faculty of the human soul does regeneration or salvation take place? Perhaps another way of posing the question is this: Where is the mechanism of choice-making in the human soul and what controls it? Please concentrate though, what is subsequently stated may seem esoteric. Trust me, it is not; actually, it is a key to the spiritual life.

While variously described, the invisible human soul may be said to be composed of two parts, understanding and inclination (what makes this difficult is that categories are not always precisely defined and demarcated, but overlap in the Scriptures). The realm of understanding is the mind, the rational faculty. The mind is a fact-gatherer that stores information; it is the gateway to the affections and subsequently the will, the faculty of action. The mind grasps ideas through the use of symbols or language. While it is vital for good decision-making that accurate information be available, the mind is not a decision-making mechanism. The mind alone can tell us that things are real, but not that they are true. Was it not Blaise Pascal who said, 'The heart has ways of knowing the mind knows not of'? For example, you can rationally know that honey is sweet without tasting it on testimony of others, but when tasted you come to know it truly to be so. The mind passes data to the conscience, which functions in making a preliminary evaluation, not a decision of acceptance, but simply the entertaining of a possibility of rejection, a flat 'No, I refuse to go there,' in most cases.

The second category of the soul is the faculty of inclination. It is composed of two faculties – affection and will. Decisions, the choice of one or another course of action, are made in the affections; often in the Bible this faculty is designated as 'the heart.' This faculty makes decisions based on a simple criterion of like or dislike, finding something either pleasurable or distasteful (all people make decisions in the same manner, saved or not). Hence, the sphere of all choices is the heart, the wellspring of the soul. Once the decision is made on the basis of minimization of pain and maximization of pleasure or delight, the will is activated and coordinated behavior follows (unfortunately, those without a true and divine understanding of pleasure, the pursuit of the holy character of God, often choose what will bring pain, thinking it leads to pleasure, and the results are negative consequences after the momentary pleasure fades). Simply stated, the will is a function of the heart, and a person's willingness is determined by the strongest motive as perceived by the mind and embraced by the affections.

The point of this discussion of the divine intrusion of the life of God is that it profoundly alters our affections, the mechanism for prioritizing what we most value at a given moment. Redemption profoundly changes forever our values and radically changes our likes and dislikes; the objects, manner, and world of what and how we love changes. Simply put, conversion alters our perspectives on life. We come to realize that there is a far greater world than this one, a world beyond the merely material that is far more beautiful, enduring, and significant than the good world of our habitation that has proven to be unfulfilling. The recognition of this invisible world has infused us with hope that will not disappoint because the object of our hope is God who longs for our presence so that we will enjoy harmony, beauty, and peace forever.

In our walk with God, it is important to know that redemption fundamentally occurs with the renovation of our affections, renewing and redefining what we love. As stated above, an effect (such as the divine life in our inner being) partakes of the character of its cause (the converse is certainly valid also: anger expressed produces resentment in return; criticism expressed produces criticism in return). The writer of the Proverbs states it this way: 'A gentle answer turns away wrath, but a harsh word stirs up anger' (15:1). Simply stated, like produces like! God is love and, thus, the manifestation of the life of God is love. 'Beloved, let us love one another for love is of God; and everyone who loves is born (literally, has been born) of God and knows God' (1 John 4:7). 'We love because He first loved us' (1 John 4:19). One of my favorite texts is how Peter describes the Christian life: '...though you have not seen Him, you love Him, and though you do not see Him now, you greatly rejoice with joy inexpressible and full of glory' (1 Pet. 1:8).

It seems that we should gather together several important thoughts that will help us as we delve deeper into the nature and mechanics of walking with God.

First, God's ultimate purpose in creation is to reveal His beauty, His glorious character often called the attributes of God.

Second, the penultimate of all of God's creation is mankind because only they share in the image of God, the capacity of intimate interpersonal communication emotionally, socially, and intellectually.

Third, God, being Trinity-in-one, desires to diffuse His presence so that He can behold His glory as well as to express it within the Trinity. Our God is a relational, community-oriented being. God likes company!

Fourth, though humanity has suffered a severe devolution from the divine purpose of creating a people that would know Him and reflect His glory, God's design for us has not been defeated or abandoned.

Fifth, God is building a community, outside the garden, a city, now piecemeal from all the nations and through all the centuries, that will one day be gathered together in the 'new heavens and the new earth.'

Sixth, God has taken the initiative to bring His intentions to fruition by reversing the effects of the great devolution. He is doing this by calling individuals to redemption through the gift of life-through-death in Jesus Christ. 'But when the fullness of time came, God sent forth His Son ...' (Gal. 4:4).

Seventh, God, who is love, revealed His love to us by sending His Son. Not only did Jesus show us the love of God, He gave His life in love for us that we might know true love. In so doing, we have found real, unsullied, unending community for the first time.

Eighth, the experience of redemption through Christ leads us to understand how much we are loved of God.

Ninth, God in our salvation has renewed and refocused our affections, what we prioritize, what we love, because He has placed His character, His love, in us.

Tenth, growing in grace, making progress in our spiritual walk, is about allowing the love of God to shine forth from our lives.

Discussion Questions

1. What are some of the implications of the fact that a life with God is more about developing character qualities than the multiplication of activities? When good activities emerge apart from character development, are we growing in our spiritual walks?

2. Why do most of us find it easier to 'do' than 'to be'?

3. According to our chapter, how does understanding the function of the Bible help you to understand the meaning of the spiritual life?

4. When God commands something of us, He provides the means and becomes the cause that makes it a reality? Is not this the meaning of grace? God says, 'I love you; I have provided for your deepest needs; I ask that you respond with appreciative obedience and reflect the glory that I have placed in you.' The religions of the world say, 'Do this and that, for you must earn my favor by doing.' How has that difference changed you?

5. What has God done to make reflecting His glory in our persons possible?

5

THE INDWELLING OF THE HOLY SPIRIT:

THE MEANS AND CHARACTER OF THE SPIRITUAL LIFE

In this section of the book, the focus has been on the divine design and enablement for the spiritual life. In essence, the spiritual life is about the cultivation of our lives in God. We began the discussion in arguing that love, by its very nature, seeks expression. All of God's actions are founded upon His character; the inter-trinitarian delight and harmony within the Godhead, the magnificent and super-abounding love of God, is the ground of all of God's creative activities. God sought to reveal His love, so that being made known it would be returned in joyful praise and willing delight expressed in praise. Not only did God create mankind, but He made men and women after His image, instilling in them a relational quality, the foundation of intimacy and communication between them and Him. Sadly, the supposed harmony between the created and the Creator was blemished, and mankind hide themselves, discovering shame instead of delight, avoiding communication with their Creator (Gen. 3:7-10). Desiring to have communion with His creation, principally His image-bearers, the Godhead devised the wonderful plan of redemption, and the restoration process, though incomplete, began.

The mechanism for the temporal process of being restored, the spiritual life, is what was specifically purchased for us in our redemption by Jesus Christ, that is the indwelling, abiding presence of the Spirit of God. It is to this third foundational act of the triune God to bring Themselves glory through the creation that we turn in this chapter.

The Holy Spirit as Divine Love

The foundation of the spiritual life is rooted in the interpersonal love of God between the members of the holy tri-unity of God. In God's essence is harmony, beauty, and loveliness. Jesus Christ, the Father's very own and beloved Equal, was through the incarnation of the love of God revealed in tangible, observable form. This love was revealed through His words and works, the culmination being His substitutionary death for us on Calvary's Tree, an act of *human* cruelty as well as profound *divine* love. '… God demonstrates His love toward us in that while we were yet sinners, Christ died for us' (Rom. 5:8). The writer to the Hebrews expressed Jesus' attitude toward Calvary, as it relates to His love for us, in this way: '… who for the joy set before Him endured the cross, despising the shame and has sat down at the right hand of the throne of God' (Heb. 12:2).

The Holy Spirit's work in the disclosure of God's love is that He is the love of God revealed through Christ and now possessed through His indwelling presence by believers. The Spirit, by regenerating every believer, is God's presence within, working to progressively make them more Christlike so that they can fulfill His calling to them to reflect or mirror the character of God. Jonathan Edwards, the famed eighteenth-century Puritan pastor in New England, spoke of the Trinity in this manner, drawing an analogy from the sun. The Father is the substance of the sun; the Son is the brightness and glory of the sun, the effervesce or shining rays; and the Holy Spirit is the experienced warmth of the sun as it enlightens, comforts and enlivens us. The Father is glory possessed, the Son is God's glory revealed, and the Spirit is the glory of God felt in the depths of our inner beings.

Reflecting upon the apostle John's first letter (principally 4:7-8, 12-13, 16), it is clear that God inhabits or indwells believers and that God is love (twice stated in these verses). Since these are verities, and the Spirit is God, then love is integral to every believer by the presence of the Spirit ('… He has given us of His Spirit'). Therefore, love is the chief characteristic of believers (the spiritual life is about ordering our lives to reflect the love of God by means of the Spirit, the 'spiritual life' being a life controlled by the Spirit of God, who is divine love). It is 'spiritual,' suggesting that its origin is beyond the world of our temporal existence. From those verses we can see several things:

First, the origin or source of love is God, the child of God bearing the imprint of her/his parent. Our love is not the cause of our relationship with God, the verb indicating that it was caused by a power outside of us (v. 7).

Second, in order to make the point even more explicit, John states it in the negative (v. 8). God, the source of begetting, is love in the sense that all of His activities are loving activities expressing the character of all His actions.

Third, if the love of God has been revealed to us (a love that God can only give to us through the gift of His very own Son, His Equal), then you and I have visible proof that we are the children of God (v. 12).

Fourth, a second ground of assurance of God's love in us is that the Spirit is present in our lives; the fact of the Spirit's presence, not the consequences of His presence merely, is a basis for assurance. To 'abide in him' in John's writings is a synonym for the possession of salvation (v. 13).

Fifth, knowing God in His very essence is to experience His love. Not so much the affection of God *for* us, but His character as love abiding *in* us (4:9, 12), though both are true, is the only ground for walking with Him (v. 16). The presence of the Spirit is the foundation of walking with God.

The Holy Spirit as the Believer's Inheritance

In discussions of the role of the Holy Spirit, it is not uncommon to focus on His activity as it relates to the application to believers of the benefits procured by Christ in His redemptive capacity. For example, we speak of the Spirit's work in opening the eyes of unbelievers to see the beauty of Christ (conviction accompanied by regeneration or rebirth), placing believers into the family of God (adoption), or uniting them to the body of Christ (Spirit baptism). What seems often neglected in the literature is that the Holy Spirit is the gift that Jesus made possible; the Spirit in us is eternal life. Thus, the Spirit of God not only applies the benefits procured by Christ, and granted by the Father, He is the benefit. It seems that in emphasizing the work of the Spirit, we have unwittingly de-emphasized the person of the Spirit in the triune, divine provision of our redemption (Eph. 1:3-14). In other words, the price of our purchase and what has been purchased with the price are of equal value. The wondrous glory that belongs to God the Father for bestowing such a salvation upon the undeserving and unmerited is the same glory expressed toward the Son for dying to make it possible, and the same glory is to be accorded to the Spirit because He is the life that has been purchased and given to us.

Biblical phrases abound for the point I am seeking to explain: '... that we would receive the promise of the Spirit through faith' (Gal. 3:13-14); '... who is given as a pledge of our inheritance' (Eph. 1:13-14); '... [God] who also sealed us and gave us the Spirit in our hearts as a pledge' (2 Cor. 1:22). The Spirit's presence within us is not verified by the ability to do the extraordinary; it is evidenced by the presence of holiness (this is why the Spirit is designated as the 'Holy' Spirit) and expressed through our moral character as love. The presence of the Spirit in the believer is the sum of the promises of God in the gospel, the sum of the saint's inheritance.

THE HOLY SPIRIT MANIFESTED IN AND THROUGH THE BELIEVER

The question before us is this: if the Holy Spirit is spirit, not material, and, therefore, not physically identifiable, how can we know that He is present within us? Being immaterial, the Spirit is not located at some particular spot within us (above the liver, in the heart, or behind the lungs); the best of technological advances in imagery cannot secure a picture of Him within us. An equally important inquiry is to answer the question, how does knowing this help us to conceptualize the spiritual life, the subject of our inquiry?

The Spirit's presence in every believer, His presence being the meaning of divine redemption (Rom. 8:9), is sometimes described as an 'abiding principle,' a 'vital principle,' 'an enduring influence,' or the 'union of the mind and heart with God Himself,' diffused through all the faculties of the immaterial soul (mind, conscience, affections, and will), and which has brought about a massive, and sudden, re-orientation of our desires, passions, and priorities. It is the life of God infused into our very beings! It is, as Jonathan Edwards has written, 'the soul's relish of the supreme excellency of the Divine.'[1]

The indwelling presence of the Spirit immediately gives the believer a sense of the loveliness, the beauty, of God's character, turning the soul from its downward drag, the plummet toward death, to the things of God and life. This indwelling is not merely a heightened moral conscience instructing me to do better; it is the loving presence of God, a sense of the loveliness of His character. It is not merely the apprehension of knowledge; it is knowledge experienced. Perhaps it can be illustrated this way: if you placed a sealed jar of something sweet before a blind person and asked him to describe what is in the container, he is not able to do so because he cannot see. However, if he tastes the contents of the jar, though blind, he can describe its content. The ability of the spiritually blind to taste and spiritually 'see' is the effect of redemption, the life-giving and indwelling presence of the Spirit of God.

Having attempted to explain the fact and nature of the indwelling presence of God, the Holy Spirit, in every believer, it seems that we can probe a little deeper by asking another question. If the Spirit's presence, being immaterial, is invisible, how can we know that He is present? Again, we may ask, why is this important for understanding the spiritual life, a life for all of us as reflective mirrors? Just as we see the branches of a tree bending, or something taken from our hands by some invisible force, and intuitively know that the wind is blowing, so it is with the presence of the Spirit of God. By the effect of something unseen, we assign an unseen cause.

---

1. Edwards defined the nature of the experience of regeneration by using a variety of terms such as 'delight' and 'relish.' For insight into his understanding of the changes in the immaterial nature of the soul, I particularly recommend two of his works: A Treatise on Grace and A Treatise on Religious Affections. These are readily available through several publishing agencies.

Galatians 5:22-23 will help in this regard: 'The fruit of the Spirit is love, joy, peace, patience, kindness, goodness, faithfulness, gentleness, self-control...' The invisible Spirit is manifested by the effect of His holy presence delineated here as nine moral character qualities. These qualities are the moral characteristics of God, the evidence of His very life within (the effect participating in the nature of its cause). Even as a child partakes of the nature of the parent, so the child of God exhibits the character of God, here called the 'fruit of the Spirit.' Thus, the effect, not the invisible essence, is the evidence.

These verses are not easy to dissect from a grammatical perspective because the noun ('fruit') and verb ('is') are singular in number while the direct object is multiple, not singular. How, then, are we to read the verse? It appears to be poor English grammar. Two options are open to us. First, we might say that the fruit of the Spirit's presence is a single collectivity composed of nine qualities. Second, we might read the verse this way: 'The fruit of the Spirit is love' and the eight qualities that follow define what love looks like practically in our daily experience.[2]

While either way to read the verse is helpful, the second seems preferable. God's essential character is love, and that love is manifested to us in the eight qualities. Love is a word that makes sense only when expressed in tangible ways! Jesus, who is the love of God revealed, manifested all of the eight qualities, and from them we have discerned that He loves us (Rev 1:5b). The Spirit is divine love possessed; we have been infused with love, which is made apparent by the eight qualities. If we want to know what love looks like, we have a description. Not

---

2. Because the language of the Greek text does not have punctuation, as in our English texts, our translators have added them to facilitate our comprehension; yet, in doing so, what they have provided is only one legitimate way to read it.

only that, we have a description of what the spiritual life should look like since the essence of a spiritual walk is love defined cogently in these eight qualities.

THE INDWELLING HOLY SPIRIT AND PRACTICAL IMPLICATIONS

If the Holy Spirit is the experience of the love of God, if the Spirit is our connection and union with Christ in love, if love in the gift of the Spirit is infused into our innermost beings becoming a new, vital principle that reshapes our priorities and values, several important implications can be drawn as it relates to the spiritual life.

First, salvation is a work of God; it is not a work of man complemented in some manner by God, nor is it the strengthening or renovating of existing talents and abilities. Simply put, redemption is the life of God in our very being. Finitude cannot produce an infinite effect by accumulating the merely finite. The divine standard of acceptance is infinite. Salvation is, and must be, the gift of God because the giver is the gift!

Second, understanding that the indwelling Spirit is the divine life, and that the essence of His presence is love, illumines us as to what it means to be in the family of God, a Jesus-follower. Love is at the heart of the Christian faith because God, the author of life, is love revealed to us through Christ by the Spirit in those eight qualities of Galatians 5:22-23. However, mere creaturely love expressed toward one another is proper, but it is not redemptive. Our love for God, and people, is not the cause of our redemption; it is the fruit of a divine intrusion by the God of heaven into our lives. That kind of love is not native to us because of our devolution; it requires infusion. It is impossible to have a love of this quality, though there are momentary vestiges of it remaining in all humans (the Bible calls it 'common grace,' the glue that holds societies together apart from redemption).

Third, if the essence of the experience of the rebirth is the infusion of the love of God into the soul, and if that love is the indwelling Spirit, it is senseless to argue that redemption does not intrinsically alter our priorities, passions, and lifestyles. Can the Holy Spirit reside in a person and deposit no evidence of His presence? While redemption is an absolutely uncaused and unmerited gift, there are consequences. Moral reformation is not to be confused with the miracle of the rebirth, but rebirth brings vast changes of perspective regarding what is to be valued.

Fourth, the consequence of love received is love willingly expressed and returned to the object that expresses it. If the character of God, which is love, seeks expression and recognition, if that love found expression in Jesus Christ, and if that love has been given to us in the gift of the divine Spirit, it is only logical that the love we have been given should seek expression as well. Again, this brings us once more to the topic before us, the spiritual life, a life ordered and disciplined to express more clearly to God the love that He has given us and to display it for others to behold.

DISCUSSION QUESTIONS

1. How has this chapter helped you to think more clearly about the resources you have been given to walk with God?

2. How would you describe in practical terms the goals or purposes of the spiritual life?

3. What is the experience of divine redemption?

4. Have you met people who claim to be Christians, but whose actions consistently and perpetually manifest the 'fruits of the flesh' (Gal 5:19-22)? What can you say about a person whose habit patterns, not mere dips of incongruity, are like that?

5. Is the endeavor to obey God, to follow His instruction, an attempt to please God or an endeavor to express appreciation for God? If God has shown His love to you, and it is infinite, can you increase or deplete it? Can you cause the love of God? What are the practical implications of the fact that you cannot?

6

THE DIVINE ORDERING OF CIRCUMSTANCES TO PROMOTE SPIRITUAL GROWTH

In the previous chapters within this section, we have sought to highlight the internal workings of God upon each of us through the Holy Spirit that are foundational to conceptualizing the spiritual life.

We have argued that knowing the reasons for God's action is important; namely, though we are a secondary means whereby God effects His primary goal, that of glorifying Himself through magnification and reflection, it is wonderful to be second when the God of the universe is first!

Moreover, God has chosen us and equipped us to be the primary means of demonstrating and reflecting His character, even above the unfallen celestial beings that stand before Him today. The manner of this accomplishment is a divine reversal of our completely fallen state through the miracle of the rebirth, the implanting of a new and divine principle within us, changing forever our priorities, goals, and passions. This new orientation is caused by the indwelling life of God, the Holy Spirit, the Spirit being the very life of God, the purchase made by the now-exalted, though once abased, Lord Jesus Christ.

In addition, the manner of the Spirit's invisible presence inhabiting and infusing Himself in all the faculties of our inner being is revealed by the display of His character through us. We have argued that God is love, love perpetually reciprocated within the Godhead. In the outworking of the multiplication and display of the mutuality of love, the indwelling Spirit is disclosing the character of the love of God, the fruits of the Spirit. If God is love, Jesus is that love revealed in incarnated form for all to see and He purchased that love for us, the Spirit being that love possessed by all believers, those who have come to embrace the person and claims of Jesus. It is the work of the triune God that alone makes the spiritual life possible, the essence of the spiritual life being love as revealed in the fruits of the Spirit.

We turn in this chapter to the external workings of God, the ordering of providence, expressed negatively and positively, giving and withholding, the joys and disappointing sorrows that equally shape us as reflective mirrors. Because God is not idle, having a purpose in all His actions of both cause and permissibility, the basic principle to have in mind is that 'it is God that is at work in you both to will and to work for His good pleasure' (Phil. 2:13). Romans 8:28 should remove all doubt about the workings of God on our behalf: 'And we know that God causes all things to work together for good to those who love God, to those called according to His purpose.'

I do not believe in randomness or luck (Ignorance, yes! Fear, yes), though I freely confess that at times I do not understand how the crushing blows of life can polish my capacity to be a reflective mirror. I am compelled to believe because of the wonder of God's benevolence through Christ which will someday deliver me from pain and death; that the first moment in heaven will be sufficient to wipe away all my bad memories, filling me with delight. I often repeat to myself an old poem, 'When answers aren't enough, there is Jesus.' I have found that greater comfort in life's dark moments is not discovered in the 'whys,' but in 'Who.' God is positively shaping each of us through positive and negative experiences to promote spiritual maturity! If God took all the rocks out of the streams that cascade down from mighty mountains, the rivers would no longer sing!

PROTECTIVE MERCIES AND PRESERVATION

Have you ever found yourself delayed in keeping an appointment by circumstances completely outside your control? Have you been delayed by a last-minute request that seemed so urgent but threatened to make you late in picking up the kids from school or athletic practice? Looking at it from our perspective, it is hard to see how disappointment could be the actual hand of God protecting us. I often wonder when being detained if God is not preventing me from being at the 'wrong place at the wrong time,' so to speak. I believe you and I have avoided mishaps, even automobile accidents, by divinely appointed delays that we conceived as a mistake, a mishap, a frightening thing.

We are under the protection of a parent who is not only wise, but supremely powerful. He is not a God who seeks to help us but is powerless to do so, nor has agedness curbed His abilities so that He now lacks perceptive powers and has become unaware of our needs. The psalmist said it more beautifully than anyone: 'I will say to my God, "My refuge and my fortress, my God in whom I trust!" For it is He who delivers from the snare of the trapper, and from the deadly pestilence. He will cover you with His pinions, and under His wings you may seek refuge; His faithfulness is a shield and bulwark' (Ps. 91:2-4).

The Book of Job deals with the problem of evil; it grapples with the question of why bad things happen to good people. Job lost it all, and his comforting friends proved anything of the sort (but at least they tried!). Job sought for answers to his heartbreak by crying out to God. Though he demonstrates remarkable faith and confidence in God – 'Shall we indeed accept good from God and not accept adversity?' (2:10), he made two mistakes in his understanding of God's ways: he accused God of not caring (chs. 38–39) and of being powerless (chs. 40–41). In the former chapters, God asks numerous questions probing of human knowledge and in the later chapters He describes two powerful beasts that He alone controls. Job ends in repentance and silence: 'Therefore, I retract. And I repent in dust and ashes' (42:6). The point is that you and I have no right to doubt or murmur in adverse circumstances simply because God is infinitely wise, powerful and loving!!

CHASTISEMENTS

Hebrews 12:5-11, which contains a citation for Proverbs 3:11-12, is, perhaps, the most poignant passage in Holy Scripture in acknowledging the fact that God is active in curbing our appetites and destructive behavior when it is detrimental to our spiritual growth, as reflecting mirrors of His glory. The Bible gives witness that adverse circumstances come to the children of God. Suffering is rooted, at least in part, in a father-son relationship (the word 'discipline' is used of training children). Some suffering is disciplinary in nature; it is part of our training to run a good 'race,' the race of life.

God disciplines us as a father does his son (v. 6), not for punishment or to express cruelty, but to prevent further destructive action on our part. This helps us to learn that negative action leads to negative consequences. Here are some old wisdom-sayings, 'People who play with fire will get burned'; 'Dance to the fiddle and you will pay the fiddler's fee.' Suffering, chastisement, and discipline are synonyms. Their presence assures us that we are in a father-son relationship with God. Chastisement, discipline, and pain in our lives are evidence that God, as a correcting, instructing Father (v. 8), cares for us. It is foolish to think that discipline is not part of God's childrearing techniques; it is part of our assurance that we are children of God. Being a daughter or son does not exempt us from suffering; it brings it. Discipline is not punishment. Punishment is payback in pain for the sake of securing justice; discipline is pain inflicted for the sake of curbing our foolishness. The motive of God is not punishment; it is remedial or corrective, though the pain seems punitive (we trust God's commitment toward us; He is our true 'Father').

DISAPPOINTMENTS

Disappointment differs from chastisements as to its origin and nature. The former is rooted in our perception of right, good, and deserving, while the latter is an act by God that has our best interest in mind. The former is found in our perception of what is best for us, while the latter is found in the infinite wisdom of God. The former is based on selfish myopia on our part ('Things did not work out as we thought they should'); in the latter God is orchestrating what is good for us. In both instances, pain is involved.

The disciples, on seeing a blind man, asked Jesus if the cause of the malady was the sin of his parents or himself, evidencing their understanding of why bad things happen (John 9:1-2). His reply is stunning; the man was born blind so that through his healing by Jesus the works of God, the claims of God, the glory of God, might be revealed (9:3). After the healing, an episode that covers an entire chapter, being a pivotal miracle in the story of Jesus narrated by John, the former blind man bears witness to Jesus' origins: 'If this man were not from God, He could do nothing' (v. 33). Even the tragedy of blindness is within God's power to cause and to use for His purposes!

You find a similar declaration by God when confronted by the reluctance of Moses to lead the people of God from Egypt (Exod. 3–4). Moses has two arguments: first, the people will not listen nor heed the Lord through him (3:11) and nor will the Pharaoh; second, he claims to be poorly endowed, not being possessed of rhetorician skills (4:10). In all the argumentation, God makes it clear that He alone will accomplish the feat for Moses. Then, we hear God say: 'Who has made man's mouth? Or, who has made him dumb or deaf, seeing or blind? Is it not I, the Lord?' (4:11).

I was raised in a rather dysfunctional home that was seemingly made more tragic when a sister, Naomi Violet, who being barely about to walk, managed to tip a pot of boiling water upon her head, scalding her severely and leaving her mentally retarded and an epileptic. It only complicated an already truncated family experience, yet that was only one of numerous factors. Why did the Lord bring into a needy family added heartbreak and sorrow? I will likely never know, but I suspect that the God who shaped my life used her life to do it. She passed from our presence a few years ago, but I still truly miss her.

While we all have different stories of our journey through life thus far, none of us will escape, nor should we, the shaping, defining, curbing influence of disappointment. If the rocks are removed from the 'river,' it would lose its capacity to sing to us!

THE EVIL ACTIONS OF OTHERS

'People hurt people' is an axiomatic truism that we all know through experience. Here I am speaking specifically about instances where others purposefully seek our harm (the robber who seeks our livelihood, the predator that steals away our youth, the critic that demeans in words and deeds destroying our right to believe in ourselves). We live in a world of security cameras, burgeoning prison populations, and an over-taxed justice system. People do hurt people; people find their significance in putting down others in dehumanized fashion. 'Sticks and stones will break my bones, but names will never hurt me,' is simply not true; it is false! Children at times, I think, would know little of unconditional trust, loyalty, or love without a dog or kitten. Why must we find security in the animal kingdom that responds only by an innate impulse? We have all been hurt by others, but could it be that God is even in that process?

Perhaps the classic example in the Bible is the outcome of the treatment of Joseph by his brothers. Caused by favoritism on the part of Jacob, resulting in sibling rivalry, jealousy, and hatred, Joseph's brothers seized the opportunity to dispatch him by placing him in a pit before figuring out how to get rid of him. While ignoring his cries, and callously taking their lunch, the brothers saw a Midianite caravan journeying toward Egypt and sold their brother into slavery. After thirteen years of imprisonment, Joseph rose to power in Egypt and later saved his people from starvation (in Egypt a family becomes a nation!).

With lies repeated, the brothers told their aching father that Joseph had been killed by a wild beast and go about their lives only to discover later that Joseph, the unwanted brother, is their only hope. However, will he seek vengeance? What did he say to his brothers when they discovered who he had become? He said, '...you sold me here; for God sent me before you to preserve life' (Gen. 45:5). After Jacob died, the brothers still had fearful consciences, but Joseph once more says, '...you meant evil against me, but God meant it for good in order to bring about this present result, to preserve many alive' (Gen. 50:20).

While we may not see how an immediate pain may promote the opposite of what traumatizes us in fear and apprehension, it may only be a matter of perspective, a perspective that can only be gained with time and distance retrospectively. If I ask you to step outside, find a tree, place your nose upon its bark, and then describe the tree, you would find it difficult simply because you would be too close to the object. However, if you stepped back fifty paces, the difficult task would suddenly become an easy one. As Jesus-followers, we may not be able to grasp with any degree of clarity the benefit of an immediate experience, frequently we only see the downside. However, with the benefit of time our perspectives often change; we come to see a 'silver-lining' in the 'garment' of disappointment and pain that encompassed us.

One rainy day, awaiting a green light, I was greatly disturbed by the fact that a college tuition payment was soon due for one of our daughters and funds were not available. Suddenly, with the road slick from a heavy rain and dark foreboding clouds obscuring vision, a car slammed into ours and, though no one was hurt, our car was written off by the insurance company. Consequently, with the insurance settlement, we had the provision of the Lord for our need. God works in wondrous ways, ways we can hardly understand at times. Ironically, I was able to purchase the car for its junk-value, repair it, and it continued to serve our needs for several years. Even in loss, there is gain if your focus is upon the Lord, but it takes time to realize it sometimes because the immediate pain and loss may be devastating.

PAINFUL SHAPING TO HELP OTHERS

God brings adverse and painful circumstances, at times, so that in our disappointment we may be given the spiritual insight and maturity to be of help to others who experience difficulties, but who are without perspective and are overwhelmed by the dark clouds of the immediate. God brings what appears to be unwanted and useless deterrents into our lives, maturing us in our faith-walk, so that we can serve and comfort others who are without the perspective gained by time and experience of following Jesus.

The apostle Paul, reminding the Corinthians of his own sufferings for the gospel, said, 'Blessed be God ... who comforts us in all our affliction so that we may be able to comfort those who are in any affliction with the comfort with which we are comforted by God' (2 Cor. 1:3-4). The 'so that' in verse 4 tells us difficulties are tools that shape us spiritually, alter our perspectives, reorientate our values, with a divine purpose. In our growth as a result of some adversity, we might be able to help others grow! Is it not a blessed comfort when we hear a friend say to us, 'I understand how you feel, I have been there'? Pain creates isolation and loneliness, but an understanding, experienced friend can change darkness into hope.

We shall forever be shaped by an experience our family endured when one of our children struggled in the midst of the horrid cycle of an active disease. We brought our daughter home from the hospital for homecare, with tubes that needed cleaning and a routine that left us weak and in despair as parents. Our daughter heard our crying one day as we sat in the living room and she came to us with the various tubes attached to her body and said with a confident tone, 'Dad and Mom, why are you crying? God gave this disease to me for His glory that I might glorify Him. Why would you take what God gives away?' Though we should have been comforting parents, spiritually matured by the decades, our nineteen-year-old comforted us with the comfort with which she was comforted and, in the process, helped us to grow spiritually!

There is an old hymn by Isaac Watts, 'Am I a Soldier of the Cross,' that goes something like this, 'Must I be carried through the skies on flow'ry beds of ease, while others fought to win the prize and sailed through bloody seas?' There are many ways that God is active to make our mirrors reflect the splendor of a world far more beautiful than this one. We are, as it were, a shapeless piece of granite, that God is chiseling and polishing into a work of artistry. There is a painful side to all of it, but sometimes there is need in our lives for refining and reshaping; God uses the 'hammer' as part of His grand scheme to hone us, as well as a gentle cloth of delivering mercies to polish us!

DISCUSSION QUESTIONS

1. Did you find it difficult to accept the fact that God is all-wise and all-powerful, but that preventable, nasty things happen to all of us?

2. What have been for you and your family sad events that in retrospect have proven to be gifts from God, outcomes that have brought blessing though initially in disguise?

3. What have you learned specifically that has made you more understanding and helpful to others? Where is the comfort you have received so that you have grown in your ability to comfort others?

4. What have you thanked God for lately because He has brought the benefit of curbing chastisement?

5. Have you come to the place that you can say with Job, 'The Lord gives and the Lord takes away, Blessed be the name of the Lord' (Job 1:21b); 'Shall we accept good from God and not accept adversity?' (Job 2:10); 'Though He slay me, I will hope in Him' (13:15)? How do you think you can get to such a place in your spiritual sojourn?

SECTION 3

POSITIVE INGREDIENTS THAT PROMOTE PERSONAL SPIRITUAL GROWTH

In the previous section, the focus was upon divine activity in the development of the Christian's walk with God. It was argued that the Lord's participation is twofold: first, the gift of God in redemption which foundationally results in a radical reorientation of the believer's affections, priorities, and passion. As a result of Christ's atoning sacrifice, the gift of life becomes the possession of the child of God, which is expressed in the gift to us of the Holy Spirit. It is the Spirit's indwelling presence that produces the fruit of the Spirit within us, with the 'fruit' being the character of God. These divine activities are internal; they are within us. Second, in the ordering of providence God is working externally to increase the reflective capacity of our 'mirrors', so that He can see Himself in us.

In this section, and the following, we turn to a discussion of the spiritual life from the perspective of the believer, the human side, discussing principles and components in our endeavor to walk with the Lord, fulfilling our calling to reflect His glory. Again, the discussion of our duty, and various mechanical components, is twofold, one is positive and the other negative. In this section, the emphasis will be upon positive activities that are integral to spiritual development.

7

THE REALIST APPROACHES
A DAUNTING TASK:

SOME PRELIMINARY OBSERVATIONS

As we approach the so-called spiritual disciplines, we realize that experience, observation and testimony make it evident that we are all strugglers. No one has neared perfection in this God-ordained task, which is our duty of conformity to the character of God, unless we have redefined sin in our lives or have become oblivious and calloused to it all. While some deal with failure by neglect, others carry around a burdened conscience, pained by inadequacies and failures. Thus, it seems appropriate, before we discuss the various means of spiritual growth, that we pause to cast the endeavor to walk with God into perspective, to speak realistically so as not to overstate the case.

THINKING ABOUT THE TASK

The spiritual life requires discipline, and discipline is the presence of habits, habits that are the fruit of training. The mature person is described in Hebrews 5:14 as one whose 'senses are trained to discern good and evil.' Habits are routines that are not easy, at least in the inceptive stage, but which over time become a delight. What we are doing by forming good habits is replacing one set of routines, perhaps better sporadic endeavors, for others. Habit-development requires determination that, with regularity and repetition, becomes integral to our daily routines.

Raised without serious preventative dental care, I have invested significant resources in fillings, bridges, and root canals over the years. At one point, my dentist invited me into his office and showed me a pair of false teeth. He introduced me to the discipline of daily flossing with the exclamation, 'Floss them or lose them, floss or prepare yourself for dentures.' I was crushed and embarrassed; a professional was being treated as a child. Faced with choices, I decided to floss. I hated it, but tried to do it daily, failing frequently. One day on a trip out-of-town, I forgot to bring my floss. I realized in missing the activity that I had developed a positive habit. It seems that good habits begin as grudging activities that over time become a delight and, hence, indispensable to our daily routines.

Lengthening of a spiritual exercise has every possibility of becoming a burden that we are not able to sustain, early in the process. It is important that we set our goals low initially and allow them to grow over time. What we value most is not necessarily what we invest most of our time doing; what we most value is what we generally think about through the day. If value is connected to the amount of time invested, then our workplace endeavors are more significant than spending time with our families; if value is connected to time investment, then repose, recreational endeavors, and sleep would be our highest values. For instance, we will likely spend over a third of our lives sleeping, yet is that a value or a necessity, like working, for the accomplishment of our values? Our values are not determined merely by time; more importantly, they are found in what we think about most. We might even become more specific; our greatest values are discovered in our involuntary thought life. What do you think about without prompting? The quality of our thoughts, the things we think about without prompting, is the gauge of our true values.

A busy mother with a time-consuming infant, other children that require finding lost items, and coordinating schedules, such as meal planning and preparation, and the maintenance of the home, has a daunting job-description. As the adage goes, 'A father works from sun to sun, but a mother's work is never done!' There simply is not time for quiet reflection (when there are always other things to do) and that can be frustrating. Moms are super multi-taskers and they know the meaning of 'tired'! Fathers are working long hours, some having commutes that leave little time through the week except to handle exigencies.

The disciplines of the spiritual life are many; managing them in a coordinated, balanced fashion is more than a rarity for all of us. The goal should be to incorporate those disciplines we find helpful and needed as we walk through the phases of our lives. Simply put, we need not be frustrated by our inability at a particular time or decade to perform a specific spiritual discipline with comfort or regularity. Some find it difficult to have an extended prayer time or to read the Bible consistently. What I have found is that as I grew older in the faith, things once difficult became easier with the change of decades, responsibilities, and physical strength. Remember life is a journey, a wonderful one, and we need to look upon it that way. 'Rome was not built in a day.' I found as a young person that fasting was not something I wanted to do or even saw the value of doing. However, as family responsibilities increased, illness and severe health needs in our children, death of family members and friends, mountain-like tasks, and debilitating disappointments, fasting became important at times. Do not be overwhelmed by what you cannot do; focus on what you can do! Children crawl before they stumble, stumble before they walk, and walk before they run!

PERSPECTIVES ON THE TASK

Do not be discouraged by the fact that you simply cannot do one or another of the disciplines, no matter how hard you try or how much resolve you muster. Think of your life as divided into decades; this has helped me. Seeing your life as a continuum in this manner should relieve a degree of your frustration, caused by failure, to rise to a level in your spiritual walk that you might idealize. The faith walk is a journey, not a sprint. What you can do when you are forty is most likely superior to what you could have done in your twenties. Perspectives change with time and circumstances (you should be far closer to the Lord in your sixties than in your thirties). If you are in your twenties, do not try to emulate someone who has walked with the Lord for over fifty years.

Time brings changes in values. Some cannot memorize Scripture; some find fasting irrelevant; some find it hard to pray in a particular fashion; and others find it hard to read the Bible daily. By personality, as well as by natural and spiritual giftedness, we are attracted to some disciplines more than others, but that also often changes over time. If you are an activist type, you might find it easier to express your devotion and worship of the Lord by serving the needs of others; if you are shy and not motivated or energized by being with people, reading may be a better outlet for you.

I find in myself that it seems that I take three steps forward and two steps backwards when it comes to spiritual progress. This is what I have found as I have struggled with disappointment and failure. So how should we respond when that happens? In three ways.

First, we must remember that walking with God is a privilege and a delight. It must be a settled conviction that we are in the family of God, that when God sees us, He sees us through the righteousness of His Son, Jesus Christ. We may see ourselves as incomplete and our actions disappointing, but He sees us clothed in the righteousness of Jesus. Says John: 'See how great a love the Father has bestowed upon us, that we should be called the children of God, and *such* we are.... Beloved, now we are the children of God, and it has not appeared as yet what we shall be. We know that, if He should appear, we shall be like Him, because we shall see Him just as He is' (1 John 3:1-2). Think of who you are in Christ. Can anyone grasp the infinite love that God has for us?

Second, do not allow the perception of the poverty of spiritual success lead you to surmise that you are not making progress. The truest barometer of progress is not merely our voluntary thoughts and actions; it is also our involuntary ones. When intuitive thoughts of care rush to your mind when seeing a need or speaking a word of encouragement to a person in trouble, that is progress. You are making progress when you catch yourself before you say or do something by asking yourself, 'Does this truly honor the Lord?' 'Does this action reveal the beauty of Christ?'

Third, progress in the spiritual life requires the perspective of time; discernment of progress is a function of time-lapse photography. Let me explain what I mean by using the illustration of a tree. Some years ago one of our sons-in-law purchased for us a tree; it was a small oak that we carried home in the trunk of a car. I have never seen the tree grow, but it has become a stately oak that dominates our backyard; my point being that growth is not always noticeable; it requires time. Further, the tree purchased for us was twisted and the trunk awkwardly bent; today it is a beautiful tree in every way. You and I are bent, twisted tiny trees, but over time we will become what we are not today. Just as the beauty of a majestic, symmetrical, well-proportioned tree reflects the beauty of its Creator, so will you and I, though our progress may not always be clearly discerned!

Some Final Comments About the Task

No one has their act together when it comes to engaging in all the spiritual disciplines. All of us have areas of spiritual success, areas needing improved discipline, and areas where we simply cannot get it together. I can assure you that the dichotomy between our public and private lives, the thoughts of our hearts and the words of our mouth, acts of omission and commission, are realities regardless of the number of years of knowing the Lord. Imagine, for example, that our spiritual lives are a house having several rooms and closets. The light of the gospel has brought light into our houses, but not consistently so. There are 'rooms' in our 'house' where shadows remain and even 'closets' that contain dark memories that we are hiding (remember, when Adam and Eve sinned, their first inclination was to hide; we build and sometimes enlarge our 'closets').

It is important for all of us that we find a discipline that we can manage within our current circumstance and begin doing it even if the steps seem staccato and abbreviated by detours, or even by poor choices. Some enjoy reading the Bible, but find it hard to memorize verses, for example. If so, I would simply read a chapter or two daily, or even just read a verse, and attempt to think through the day about what I had read. Some find a regimented time of prayer difficult, but we can pray through the day as needs come to our minds.

It is important to keep continually before us that the spiritual life is a love relationship, far more than a list of 'do's' and 'do nots'. The quest for conformity to the object of one's affections, in our case the God of infinite beauty and grace, is not a function of 'I just must do it' as it is 'I want and desire to do it.' It is not about how well we are doing; it is about respect and delight that brings with it a compelling passion of conformity because we have been forgiven our sins and given hope by the Lord. Love is more than an emotion, subject to circumstance and time; it is a state of being. That state for us is the presence of the life of God, the Holy Spirit, in our very beings. My thoughts can be summarized in the words of John: 'Beloved, let us love one another, for love is from God, and everyone who loves is [the sense being, "has been already"] born of God and knows God. The one who does not love does not know God, for God is love. By this the love of God was manifest in us, that God sent His only begotten Son into the world so that we might live through Him' (1 John 4:7-9).

By personality and spiritual giftedness, we are naturally given to some disciplines more than to others. I am convinced that a lot of how we manifest our spirituality is rooted in our natural makeup. If you are given to activism, finding it hard to sit quietly with little to do, you are likely to express your love for the Lord through service to others. If you are a people-person, energized by being with others, you might find it natural to share your religious opinions. If you are shy, you may be able to excel in the quiet disciplines of prayer, meditation, or reading. Much of spirituality is shaped by personality!

The goal of our walk with the Lord should be to incorporate as many of the disciplines as possible. There is a tendency to emphasize what we are better at doing, rather than disciplines that are harder for us (actually, in order to justify the presence of undeveloped virtues we excuse ourselves by thinking that one or another discipline can cancel out the necessity of others). Further, there is a tendency to judge the spiritual progress of others by the measure of our spiritual accomplishments. I often think of the spiritual life as that of the juggler's trade, one who seeks to entertain by artfully keeping a number of balls simultaneously in the air. For an accomplished juggler, it might be easy to keep five balls going; for the novice, three is a challenge. The spiritual life has many components or activities. Some may be able to juggle more 'balls' than others, but there are more 'balls' than any of us can handle with consistency. If there are eight 'balls' (I am only using this number to make my case) that we all need to juggle, the task is to not only get them off the floor, but to keep them all at the same height and intensity. The goal of our spiritual endeavors should be to incorporate as many disciplines as we can manage through the experiences of our lives. Do not be discouraged by what you cannot do, for we all drop 'balls' in this life; delight in what you can do and in the progress you can see over time. This is not a 'bead counting endeavor'; it is the unfolding and deepening of a love relationship.

DISCUSSION QUESTIONS

1. One of the positive things about nurturing our spiritual life is that we are all different; we each have strengths and weaknesses. This means that we all need help and we all are able to help struggling sisters and brothers in

Christ. This mutual interrelatedness is the community aspect of Christian growth. Have you found this to be true?

2. How do you think you can turn an activity that is a drudgery into a delightful habit in your life?

3. How has understanding that we are all on a journey, a journey that will stretch over decades and that progress is possible through the aging process, helped you?

4. How does spirituality differ from Christian maturity? If a novice in the Christian disciplines can be spiritual, though they may not be mature, what does that help us to understand?

5. In what ways has this chapter-discussion encouraged you and challenged you?

8

THE MIND AND THE SPIRITUAL LIFE

We have argued previously that the soul is composed of two faculties, the intellectual and the inclinational. Further, we have suggested that within the latter, decisions or choices are determined by the sub-faculty of the affections – the mechanism that evaluates the propriety of the data presented to it, whether it conceives it as valuable or not – engaging the will which then calls for consequent action, and it is done.

The choice-determining affections are dependent on accurate information being delivered to them, as well as by an inwardly developed intuitive sense of what is good and what is not; poor and inaccurate data leads to damaging decisions. Have we not all been disappointed by promises that were too good to be true, and they were not! Simply put, the mind, our facts-gathering faculty, is crucial to decision-making. What one allows into their minds will shape and determine their choices. Good choices result from good input!

How do I determine what to think about, what to mentally entertain, if the Christian life is so vitally connected to mental activity? A Bible verse I often think of is Philippians 4:8: '... whatever is true, whatever is honorable, whatever is right, whatever is pure, whatever is lovely, whatever is of good repute, if there is any excellence and if anything worthy of praise, dwell on these things.' This seems to be a litmus-test text of how we can determine the criteria of what we should be preoccupied with mentally. Being in the capacity of an advice-giver, I am often asked about choices. What I often say is this: 'Can you think of it without violating the criteria of Philippians 4:8?' If you cannot, you will be without the peace of God in your decision. Walking with God requires right choices; right choices depend upon the acquisition of wholesome information.

Two other comments of Paul come to my mind at this juncture, emphasizing the importance of what we expose our minds to receive. In Romans 8:6, he draws a contrast between unwholesome ideas and destructive ones without mentioning particulars: 'For the mind set on the flesh is death, but the mind set on the Spirit is life and peace.' What we entertain mentally, what we allow ourselves to think about, what we meditate upon, has definite outcomes. To be spiritually minded means to have our inclinations, disposition, and frame of mind set on the things of heaven. It is a delight or relish for such things. It is this that separates the regenerate from the unregenerate, and it promotes spiritual life and peace.

The second comment is more than a statement of fact; it is a command: 'Set you mind on the things above, not on the things on the earth' (Col. 3:2). The battleground for the affections, which is the root of all action, is the mind, the mental, the reservoir of stored available data. Walking with God, what biblical scholars refer to as sanctification, begins with right thoughts.

THE SOURCE OF GOOD IDEAS

We live in an increasingly secularized culture which is the result of an intellectual assault upon the Christian faith that became increasingly potent in the eighteenth century, and which was propelled by the rise of the sciences and which became increasingly dominant in the universities, and which has reduced the notion of what is real to naturalism and materialism. This movement that promised to reverse the savagery of the human past through mathematics, science, and technology has accomplished many wonderful advances across numerous disciplines. However, the cost of material advance has been at the tragic impoverishment, if not complete neglect, of the immaterial human soul and the realities of a world greater than this one – heaven. The promise of redemption through technology has left us with much, but little of meaning; we now have the confusion of activities and of status with significance (the meaning of life is now often determined by wealth access, physical attractiveness, and athleticism). With the collapse of this centuries-old endeavor at human redemption, increasingly relegating God to the realm of fringe-relevance and hell to myth, the project fell to pieces under the onslaught of its own massive success, the sad accompanying consequence of holocausts in the past century, and growing insecurity in this one. We have become so busy in being busy that the family, the most fundamental unit of society, is in jeopardy of disintegration through broken promises and dysfunctional parenting techniques. Unfortunately, and unnecessarily, the loss of truth and moral integrity has come at the cost of social advancement. The glue of any culture is shared values. However, we find ourselves left with only individual rights and those rights are determined by the individual! Pleasure, the quest for immediate gratification, has brought to us a society of anarchists and exploiters.

What does all of this have to do with the topic of walking with God? If my assumption is correct that values and subsequent behaviors are determined by what we accept as true and worthy, then accurate information is of utmost importance to wise and appropriate decision-making. Simply put: Good input is crucial to making good decisions.

Because we are living in a culture that has rejected the realities of God and the wisdom of the Bible, the increasing tendency is to only be alert to sources of input or advice of a naturalistic, personal, or materialistic origin. While information is needed and somewhat helpful, it is often incomplete and twisted, and therefore dangerous. There is more available knowledge than what we can acquire through the wisdom of trusted friends, family, educators, or trustworthy professional counselors. As Christians, perhaps a better term these days is Christ-followers, we live with a set of assumptions and values that are not shared by those who have not made such commitments. Let me explain something about our values that has led us to believe that the sum of human wisdom is incomplete, sometimes even dangerous.

First, we believe that there is a world beyond our physical sight that is more real, more enduring, and more beautiful than the world we currently inhabit. We fundamentally embrace the idea of the existence of a God who dwells in a world untouched by human imperfection with adoring angels and with the souls of believers who have departed this life and who in the resurrection at the end of days will receive a new body with which to dwell in the presence of God forever. We are a people motivated by a hope that the unseen is more real than the seen!

Second, we believe that God is not only the creator and maintainer of all things, but His character is the singular standard of ethics. He is right and perfect in all His attitudes, which are always consistent with His actions. Therefore, cultural values, as we experience them, at best reflect His character and, at worst, are in contradistinction to His character. As radical as it sounds, majority consensus, governmental decrees verified by the justice system, and social scientists (social workers, psychiatrists, and psychologists) are only trustworthy to the degree that they reflect and communicate the values and morals resplendent in the character of God.

Third, we believe that every human being, female or male, has suffered a serious retrogression, though not a complete denouement of the rational faculties, and that we have become gullible to the attractiveness of misinformation that feeds the promise of our pleasures. Not only is this so, but the environment in which we live has been punctured. The created world of flora and fauna itself has suffered relapse from its created ideal and purposes. To make matters worse God has permitted the operation of the world, in a limited and temporal sense, to be under the governance of the diabolical. We find ourselves in a grand impasse; we lack the ability to know God, to embrace intellectually the depth of His character; there is no ladder long enough that we can climb to reach the dwelling presence of God!

Fourth, the above being the case, we believe that God has condescended to us so that we can have insight into Him. How can even the best of men and women rise to the standard of the acceptance of God when the standard is God Himself? What the Fall destroyed, grace has restored! Typically, when it comes to the sources of the knowledge of God, we think of three or four venues: the incarnation of God in Jesus Christ, a person; the Bible, the words of God; tradition, the collective wisdom of the past; and, for some a separate category, experience, the spiritual and personal intersection and interaction with Christ, the Bible, and us. Of these four valued sources, one is a person who stands supreme because He alone is the 'Word of God' (1 John 1:1-4). Having said this, the person of God in Christ, the living Word, and the written Word, the Bible, are distinguishable, but inseparable. Our knowledge of Jesus Christ has come to us through the written Word, the Bible, by the illuminating and regenerating ministry of the Spirit. These three – Christ, the Bible, and the Holy Spirit – are the embodiment of our knowledge of God (Jesus revealed God to us in His person, being God in the flesh), the Bible is the literary description of God, whom Christ revealed, and delivered to us in written form by the writers of Holy Scripture. The Holy Spirit superintended the writing so that the product reflects a single divine purpose consistent with the divine perfections of His character.

This does not mean, however, that all the resources of divine instruction for our lives that God has made available to us, to help us walk wisely, are of the same, seamless, and impeccable quality. These other sources are categorized under the term, 'Natural Revelation.' Unlike the Bible or Christ, both administered to us by the Holy Spirit (being holy the Spirit cannot act in an unholy manner because God cannot act contrary to Himself), these are incomplete, imperfect, or somewhat sullied sources. 'The heavens declare the glory of God' (Ps. 19:1-2), though they tell us little beyond His majestic existence and power. The consciences of all people, an intuitive sense of right and wrong, are wonderful, but that sense is not powerful enough to overcome their moral blindness and self-will. The instruction of the wisdom of the past, the collective wisdom of sages, have come down to us as literary-source materials for our edification and instruction. And finally, we are all surrounded by friends, counselors, and pastors, some who know us better than others, but who are wonderful sources of common sense and, often, deep spiritual insight relative to the issues that confront us, often on a daily basis.

THE PLACE TO BEGIN: GOOD INPUT AND A CAUTION

The path to good decision-making begins with good options. Simply put: rarely does inaccurate information lead to good decisions on our part, but the accurate presentation of facts and their implications do. We live in a culture wherein the news media, be it electronic media, newsprint, or the evening news, is often narrowly biased. That needs little verification, but the point stands that even in a world of twisted, distorted messages, information is vital.

However, the availability of good choices, and even choosing a good option to pass on for the affectional faculty to select, does not make the option, in itself, good. Good ideas alone are not the path to honor God in our lives for His unexpected, even shocking, display of kindness and grace. What makes an action pleasing to God is not the act in itself but the motive behind the act. If the opposite were the case, fine moral people would have a claim to heaven and it could be obtained by people we know who have better morals and life-skills than some. One of my teachers said to me one day, as I was disputing the claim that all good people have a right to heaven, 'There is more common grace in some unbelievers than there is special grace in some believers (meaning, some non-Christians have better morals than some Christians), but it is not the amount of special grace that makes one a Christian.' Morals are not the ground of the hope of heaven; divine grace is; and the grace that purchased the right of heaven for us is apart from works and only through faith in Jesus as a person and in what He accomplished on Calvary's tree. 'Without faith it is impossible to please Him, for he who comes to God must first believe that He is and that He is a rewarder of those who seek Him,' noted the writer of Hebrews (11:6). True belief or trust in the Lord has three components. First, it consists in *assent* that certain claims and facts are real about Jesus. Second, it consists in the recognition that those certain, real facts are true. However, these two facets of faith do not make one a Christian; even the devil knows this much. The third element is *trust or reliance* upon those true and real facts. This affectional embrace, trust, reliance, and commitment is what is key to receiving God's redemption. Faith consists of assent and consent!

I write this as we begin our discussion of the disciplines related to walking with God to emphasize the point that it is not about a list of things to do; it is about the expression of a relationship of love, fellowship, communion, and delight in God. Christianity is concerned about right actions, but not moralism; the path to heaven is called 'the way of faith' and is opposed to self-accomplishment. The disciplines in themselves are somewhat mechanical; the authenticity comes out of the motive for their expression, mainly gratitude for the purchased-for-us grace of God by the Lord Jesus.

A WAY TO ORGANIZE THE TASK: WALKING WITH GOD

In reading the literature on the topic of walking with God, I have come to conclude that a rich heritage of thoughts can be found by turning the pages of our Christian past. I have found a richness in the literature of the sixteenth and seventeenth centuries that is helpful, particularly that of the English Puritan tradition. I have found this to be so because the religious emphases of that era were more God-focused than the Christian cultures of the present. Today, the questions answered in the literature have more to do with life-management issues (my life, positive feelings, and immediate outcomes) than underlying causes of dysfunction and stress. To be more specific, the English and Scottish reformers understood two biblical concepts that seem to be given only cursory reflection today. The first of these is the holiness, majestic awesomeness, and glorious beauty of God. Much of modern expressions of Christianity seem preoccupied with the compassionate, intimate friendliness of God, making Him appear more like us than Himself. The second is that our forebears understood the gravity of the human condition as more profoundly marred than is understood today. With a culture that emphasizes quick solutions to complex issues in our lives, the realism of echoes from the past seems deeply refreshing. I am reminded of a verse from Jeremiah the prophet: '...ask for ancient paths where the good way is, and walk in it and you will find rest for your souls' (Jer. 6:16).

The discussion of the spiritual life that follows has two aspects: some positive steps and some negative actions. The positive side deals with those disciplines that promote good, wholesome input, sources that shape our minds and mental attractions. The negative actions have to do with how to go about dealing with sin in our lives. In previous centuries, the former was described by the word 'vivification,' meaning things that promote spiritual health; the latter was denominated by the word 'mortification,' meaning putting to death inappropriate actions and attitudes that only are destructive to spiritual health. Perhaps, a verse that we might use to summarize the quest for positive input is 2 Peter 3:18: 'But grow in grace and the knowledge of our Lord and Savior Jesus Christ ....' Perhaps even more declarative is 2 Peter 1:5-7: '... apply all diligence: in your faith, supply moral excellence; and in your moral excellence, knowledge; and in your knowledge, self-control; and in your self-control, perseverance; and in your perseverance, godliness; and in your godliness, brotherly kindness; and in your brotherly kindness, love.' As to the negative in sanctification, dealing with the darkness in all of our souls, the things that rob us of peace and trouble our consciences, perhaps Romans 8:13, which is both an exhortation and a promise, is much to the point: '... if you, by the Spirit, are putting to death the deeds of the body, you will live.'

DISCUSSION QUESTIONS

1. With our culture's preoccupation with the enjoyment and improvement of one's existential existence or experience of life now, do you think this accounts for a decline of interest in heaven? In contemporary Evangelicalism, is there a link between the decline of religious vitality in our churches and a commensurate preoccupation with life now?

2. Can you have authentic Christianity without an emphasis on eternal hope? Is the best way of showing the compassion of Christ to express faith that is more

preoccupied with doing good to our neighbors, and pursuing social justice, than meditation on the beauty of Jesus? Is there a danger in moralizing the Christian faith? While a balance seems valid, has the balance become an imbalance? Can social justice be maintained when devotional piety is confused with it?

3. Has the emphasis in Christian Faith in the West shifted from an emphasis on character and moral integrity to an emphasis on productivity and culturally defined definitions of success? It seems that you can have serious religious success, a growing church, without a growing preoccupation with the beauty of the Savior. Have you begun to think that a heart set on heaven, a mind focused on worship, is your chief calling as a follower of Jesus? Have you allowed to go unquestioned a cultural definition of a successful life?

4. Do you consciously think about the beauty of the Savior in His person, offices (prophet, priest, and king), and grace? Do you have a mind set on heaven and the exalted Redeemer or are you preoccupied with managing life wisely? If the meaning of success is 'more' and 'greater,' you and I will end our lives in disappointment. What are you doing to prevent that?

5. The key to the spiritual life is what controls and activates our affections. A mind set on Jesus Christ is a life that is successful regardless of the vicissitudes and turns of life. You simply cannot be preoccupied with two things at the same time. What you allow yourself to think about will affect your affections and consequently your will or choices. Are you guarding your mind? Are you feeding it with a proper diet?

6. Do you understand that in a blighted world our existence will never be without blight? While we strive to create the perfect world by building our walls to keep people and hurts out, it will not work. In fact, that approach to pain-relief has only proven to create more pain because community, not isolation, is the key to healing. We need the inter-trinitarian community of the Godhead as well as the community of friends. A perfect world awaits us through our perfect Savior, Jesus Christ. What are the practical implications of this for your life, family, and ministry?

9

Right Thoughts Require Good Input:
The Place of the Bible

As we enter into a discussion of the disciplines of the spiritual life, the biblical directives and activities sanctioned by Holy Scripture, it is easy for all of us to feel guilty because none of us are all that we should be. We all have our shortcomings. The chasm between 'ought' and actuality troubles all our consciences; we can talk far more accurately than we live! Because I have come to realize that walking with God on an intimate basis is the result of a love relationship, experiencing the realities of how much God truly loves His children, the issue is not a list of 'do this, do that.' What I am entering into with you now is not to make you uneasy with your inabilities; rather, it is to make progress in learning how much God is committed to us because His love is infinite and without blemish, inadmissible of increase or decrease. Human dereliction does not alter family affiliation!

As we think about the cultivation of our spiritual dimension, the other side of the mundane and routine, there are a few things to keep in mind. First, walking with the Lord is more of an endurance race, using a metaphor from track and field, than a sprint or one-hundred-yard dash. While you and I can be instantaneously spiritual, meaning rightly related to the Holy Spirit through His indwelling presence, spiritual maturity is not; it requires time, experience, and perseverance. There is an old adage, 'Rome was not built in a day,' a fitting analogy in the path toward godliness with contentment. For most of us, the deed to our homes resides in a bank for twenty or thirty years before we can truly claim ownership; good things take time and effort.

Second, remember that the goal is progress, not perfection. As we will explain in the next section, our death to sin in Christ is not universal; the guilt and penalty of sin has been fully paid, yet the presence of sin has not been eradicated (if you believe your behavior is flawless, you have a lot of explaining to do and much that you cannot explain in the church). The issue is not doing something to perfection; it is seeking to do what is right. What I have come to realize is that the only thing consistent in my life is inconsistency. None of us can get it right all the time; none of us are adept at employing all the disciplines of the spiritual life. This is why we all need each other.

Third, progress in spiritual growth is not always discernible, or even quantifiable; indeed, it may be internal more than external at times. Change requires an alteration of ideas and values; change is simply the fruit of what we invisibly have come to prioritize. It is the application of insight!

Fourth, when we stop doing what we should, we should simply start over again. The spiritual disciplines seem to be like the cycle of the seasons; they ebb at times and are renewed at others. Henry Ford said it well, 'Success is progressing from one failure to the next without a loss of enthusiasm.' You may fail, but do not quit!! The chief characteristic of the saint's life is not how well we are doing, but what we do when we are not doing well.

READING THE WORD OF GOD

If you desire to think good thoughts, you must have good ideas in your mind (good options lead to the possibility of good choices). You simply cannot avail yourself to what is not present; however, good ideas are available. Advice-givers are not hard to find, but in this life, you will not find one individual who is impeccably wise, immensely intelligent, unblighted by the prevarications of broken humanity, altogether concerned for us, and truthful without exception. There is One who is all those things and more, the creator and preserver of all things, the almighty God who spoke complexity into existence with no depletion of energy, the One revealed to us in the Lord Jesus, the One we have come to know through the Holy Spirit, the One who gave us in our language a disclosure of His character, power, and love so that we could hold it in our hands, read its pages, and ponder its unfathomable wisdom for all our needs.

The Bible is indispensable in our walk with God; how can you companion with someone when you are unwilling to spend time in their presence? How can we say that we are loved by the God of heaven and not seek to bask in the beauty of it all? How can we lay aside the great book by the greatest of all authors, the book that addresses the deepest needs of humanity (to be forgiven and to be loved in an unrelenting manner), the book that has brought unspeakable comfort in our greatest distress, and not consult it regularly? When you are troubled by unwholesome thoughts and gruesome fears, have you not found in the Bible the soft breeze in the midst of the storm? Why is the Bible so very important? It describes for us the wonder of our redemption through the Lord Jesus. No other book in all the world has been written by God; it is the declaration of the love of God, the covenantal faithfulness of God, the sureness of all the promises of God. There is no other book like this one! The Psalmist said it this way: 'Your word is a lamp to my feet, a light to my path' (119:105), and then 'Your testimonies are wonderful; therefore my soul observes them. The unfolding of Your words gives light; and understanding to the simple' (119:129-30). Jesus made the point succinctly, 'Your word is truth' (John 17:17).

While the Word of God is indispensable for the revelation of God, our calling to God through Jesus Christ, instruction for walking with God, and the hope of someday being in the very presence of God, what can we say about relating to the Bible in our walk with God now? Clearly, you and I cannot walk with God without connecting ourselves to His Word. Here are a few thoughts.

First, it is not about the length of time you spend in reading the Bible daily; it is about frequency of doing so with a listening ear and repentant heart. How much you choose to read is not the point. By reading three chapters a day you can make it through the Bible yearly. Others read a paragraph or even a single verse (spirituality is not a product of any specific technique; it is about sincerity, humility, submission, and passionate delight). A busy housewife with little ones tugging at her shirt, lunches to pack, lost things to find, a house to keep in order, a husband to console (the list is endless), hardly has any durative quiet time for reading. It is not about how much you read; it is about the development of the habit of reading the Bible.

Second, successful Bible reading is not about remembering what you read; we are all frustrated that we have read the Bible, been exposed to it through many venues, and, yet, it seems that we have forgotten more than we have learned. In the world of mechanics, progress is often identified by tangible criteria; however, in the realm of spiritual development, progress cannot always be empirically identified because growth is often more attitudinal than mental storage. Not all growth is cognitive; in fact, the most important is in the realm of attitudes, values, and desires.

Third, regardless of the length of reading in any given day, do so slowly and meditatively, asking yourself the meaning of the text and how it applies to whatever you are facing. I have found it helpful to ask two questions in my reading. First, what does this text tell me about my Savior? Second, I ask of the text, 'What comfort can I derive to deepen my relationship with Him?' Bulk reading is not always the best; think not about how to lengthen your reading, but how to deepen your understanding of what you have read.

Fourth, there are times when reading is difficult for us simply because of the crunch of things that goes on in our lives. Some people find it hard to sit and read; some are simply not readers. If that is true of you, you can obtain the Bible in electronic form and listen to it being read. That is a wonderful way to fill your mind with good thoughts and to think of the things of the Lord. Most of us drive to work; why not utilize the time by listening to the Bible! Most of us have audio facility in our homes.

As to further options, some find it more comfortable to read a daily devotional guide that cites a verse or two followed by reflective comments. The point is that you should do what you find consistent with your personal makeup coupled with your immediate situation. Activist types find it hard to sit quietly. I have realized that much of what we practice as spiritual disciplines has a great deal to do with our heritage and personalities. Find something that suits you, that you find comfortable doing, and, over time, you will see spiritual growth and development. The issue is the development of routines that become habits!

THINKING ABOUT THE WORDS FROM GOD AND THE GOSPEL

Good thoughts require not only the possession of good ideas, but the imbibing of them. Whatever the length of the reading for the day, allow time to think, ponder, reflect upon what you have read; what I am talking about is the art of meditation. Do not merely read so that you can say that you have read (rituals are not the same as ritualism; so use your reading as a springboard for the day). The first of the psalms says it this way, 'How blessed is the man who does not walk in the counsel of the wicked .... But his delight is in the law of the Lord and in his law does he meditate day and night' (Ps. 1:1-2). Elsewhere the psalmist wrote, 'When I remember You on my bed, I meditate on You in the night watches' (Ps. 63:6). Here are some clues regarding how to do this.

First, from your reading you might select a key verse or two, even a general idea that struck you, and try to think about it in those random instances throughout the day when you have a moment or an involuntary thought darts across your mind (often these are not planned moments but with practice they, being lodged in the subconscious, bubble to the surface). Thinking good thoughts is a bulwark against the intrusion of destructive, unhelpful thoughts. For example, my reading today was in Acts 16. I was impressed by the moral and attitudinal changes that came about when God opened the heart of a jailor. The passage offers wonderful insight into the change salvation brings. From throwing Paul and Silas into an inner prison, caring not for their wounds, the jailor became a concerned caregiver taking them into his home, binding their wounds, and offering food and fellowship. What a picture of redemption! He and his household were filled with joy, although hours earlier he had felt that suicide was a better option than Roman justice!! What does this episode, this timeless episode, tell you and me while shuffling papers, taking a break, doing dishes, driving to pick up the kids, taking a shower or hot bath, or sitting on the back porch after a long day?

Second, it is helpful to write out a text of Scripture and place it where it can be easily seen such as near the sink, on the refrigerator, the dashboard of the car, or by your favorite chair. Things that remind us to be mindful are helpful!

Third, do not allow yourself to read so much that you do not have time to think about what you are reading. A spoon holds a small amount of water, but the cumulative effect of spooning can fill a bucket. In the world of finances, the cumulative result of simple compounding is amazing with the perspective of a decade or two.

Fourth, I have found it fruitful, devotionally inspiring, to quietly reflect on the message of the Bible as a whole, to think more broadly than a particular verse or chapter. The Bible discloses to us the character of the triune God; it is a love story, the story of God's great condescending love and covenantal faithfulness to gather a people to adore and worship Him forever. It is a profitable experience to think about the grace and wonder of the redemption that God has brought to us – it brings delight and comfort to our hearts. The old hymn-line, written by Helen Lemmel (1864–1961), speaks volumes when it says,

> Turn your eyes upon Jesus,
> Look full in His wonderful face,
> and the things of earth will grow strangely dim
> in the light of His glory and grace.[1]

1. I have taken the poem from *Great Hymns of the Faith* (Grand Rapids: Zondervan Corporation, 1974), 204.

The following are only examples illustrating what may be profitable to meditate upon in moments of reflection as you make it a habit to think purposefully and pointedly about the Lord. When you have those moments of spiritual focus, often quite brief, think of the love of God for you. Think of His love as an ever-flowing bounty of affection; He adds to us by His love; we add nothing to Him by ours. Think on the Father's love as antecedent love, our love as subsequent love, and what that truly means. We love because He first loved us. Our love must have an object, so it must have a cause (causeless objects do not exist). Reflect on how much God loves you because His love, like all His actions, is an outflow of His character, His perfections.

Take a few moments as you drive along in your car to focus on Jesus. Allow your mind to delight in the wonder of His condescension. 'O the love that drew salvation's plan, O the love that brought it down to man.' Contemplate for a moment the wonder of Calvary, the payment of our debt and its tremendous cost, but also His willing sacrifice for us: '… who for the joy set before Him, endured the cross, thought despising the shame' (Heb. 12:2). Think of the implications for you of His defeat of sin and death, His glorious triumph, His intercession for us as our great high priest, and His glorious reign as King of Kings and Lord of Lords today and forever.

Contemplate upon the ministry of the Holy Spirit in His roles as comforter, guide, and teacher. It is the Spirit who applies the benefits of Christ's purchase to us; He is the One who brought life to us. It is the indwelling Spirit of God who is our assurance that we are indeed the children of God, having sealed us with Himself (Eph. 1:13), driving away our fears and doubts. We should not merely worship the Spirit because He is our comforter/helper, the

'Another' promised by Jesus in His absence (John 14:16, 26; 15:26); He is our God!

MEMORIZING THE WORDS OF GOD

In a great psalm that celebrates the Word of God, the psalmist wrote these immortal words: 'With all my heart I sought You; do not let me wander from Your commandments. Your word have I treasured in my heart that I might not sin against You' (Ps. 119:10-11). Putting the Word of God in our minds is not an option; it is a mandate. When I read the New Testament, it is shocking to me that some one third of it is composed of quotations, the recall of events, and echoes from the Old Testament, the Hebrew Scriptures. The writers of the Greek Scriptures were people that had a deep grounding in their Bibles, so much so that they had facility to quote it prolifically. Filling our minds with the Bible is not a mere luxury; it is life-changing. It is the path of transformation 'by the renewing of your mind' (Rom. 12:2).

Memorizing is the road to remembering and recalling, whether it be a verse from the Bible that we learned early in our Christian experience or hymns that we sang as children. Remember, we are likely to be governed by what we think about because information is the fertile ground out of which the seeds of choice-making grow and flower. With regard to the disciplines, each of us relates to them differently and in a varying manner over the decades. Some find it hard to memorize Scripture; it is not essential, an all or nothing deal, but it, like the others, is exceedingly helpful.

If you sought to memorize one verse a month, you would manage twelve a year and in ten years, with time to review as you go along, you would have one hundred and twenty verses in your memory bank. All of us could focus on one verse a month. I write this example to make the point that a little over time can amount to a lot!

As we conclude this chapter, I would like to throw out a challenge, and with it, make a promise to you, though I am not a prophet nor the son of a prophet (it is made out of the fund of personal experience). If you read three chapters of the Bible daily, you can read its entirety in a year. If you read the Bible through in a succession of years, say three, you will have immersed yourself in the Word of God and you will involuntarily think of its content as you experience the throes and joys of life. If you memorize just twelve verses a year, with the extensions of years, you will see a transformation in your thought-life.

DISCUSSION QUESTIONS

1. When you think about the disciplines explained in this chapter, which one do you think is the easiest for you? Why do you think that is so?

2. What do you think are the greatest hindrances in your life that make these disciplines hard at times?

3. What have you found that has been a help to you as you have tried to have a consistent walk with the Lord?

4. If none of us are all that we should be in our walk with the Lord, how do you handle the guilt that often comes when you hear that, in a particular area, others are doing better than you?

5. Have you allowed weakness in the development of one or another discipline to justify those that are easier for you and further your neglect to improve?

6. Are you willing to accept one of the challenges that concluded the chapter? What behavior modifications will you need to make to take on the challenge? When intimacy with God is the highest privilege of the child of God, is there a reason not to avail ourselves of the means to do so?

10

RIGHT THOUGHTS REQUIRE GOOD INPUT:
THE IMPORTANCE OF PRAYER

In essence, prayer is a many-faceted conversation with God, addressing not only our needs, our plight, and certainly those of others, but far more. It is an act of submission and recognition that God is our sustainer and provider, an act declaring dependence. The Westminster Larger Catechism defines prayer as 'offering our desires to God' (Q 178); the Heidelberg Catechism defines prayer as the 'chief part of thankfulness which God requires of us' (Q 116). It involves both adoration and worship as we intellectually and emotionally enter into the presence of God, voicing our concerns for the extension of His work in the world and, thereby, participating joyfully in it. Prayer, in essence, is verbalizing our thoughts to God as the focus of our communication with One who is alone most-powerful, and, thus, able to answer our requests, and most-caring, suggestive of His delight to do so.

PRAYER BAFFLES US, BUT IS ESSENTIAL
There is something strange about prayer, a considerable conundrum of sorts. First, for example, the posture of prayer often takes place in stark contrast to the consequences of beseeching our prayer-answering God.

Often we bow, with closed eyes and hands folded, unaware of the circumstances that surround us, defenceless in the presence of an adversary should one lurk close by, and yet it is a time of refreshment and delight beyond measure.

Second, there are several words in the New Testament for prayer and collectively they carry the notion of asking, beseeching, requesting, or making supplication. Yet, prayer is far more than presenting a detailed list of wants and needs; it is an avenue through which we can cultivate wholesome communication while delighting in the presence of the Lord. Prayer is entering into fellowship with the God who delights to hear His children explain to Him their thoughts, passions, disappointments, and challenges.

Third, the mystery of how prayer works is also befuddling to our minds. How does God answer our prayers that require Him to act before anyone asks, setting into sequence a course of events that require significant pre-planning and execution? If God has a perfect knowledge of all things, controls all things, and determines all things, why is prayer a crucial component in the spiritual life as clearly instructed by and exemplified in the life of Jesus? How can it be that we do not have because we do not ask, since we do not receive simply because we ask, and the sequence of events required to answer our requests takes place prior to our asking (often God working in other people's lives who are the medium of God's answer)? Our prayers never match the mercies that God extends to us daily, with or without our request or pleas.

An analogy relative to the incomprehensibility of prayer may be that of an ant walking across a great painting such as Leonardo's 'Mona Lisa' (1503), Rembrandt's 'The Lifting of the Cross' (ca. 1633), or Monet's 'Water Lilies' (1906). Crawling across a canvas, the ant might observe an array of brilliant colors, even pausing to recognize the changing hues, but the overall picture would be beyond its grasp. This is because a lack of perspective prevents proper assessment and appreciation. That is how it is with prayer. It is integral to the Christian life, being an ingredient in spiritual health and a command of God. It is an act of submission that defies our understanding. (We believe that there is a greater, more beautiful world outside of the limitations of the sphere in which we live. Additionally, we believe that God is infinite wisdom and knowledge and we are myopic, blighted creatures. We should find it foolish to limit God by our limited knowledge.)

Prayer: Rooted in the Redemptive Experience

Foundationally, prayer is grounded in the character of God and in the infusion of the divine life through the redemptive experience in which we received God's divine acquittal on the basis of divine justice met for us through Christ's acceptance of and payment for our sins, and its application by the Holy Spirit. Thus, the manner of unpacking the nature of God is to understand the nature of salvation, the two being intrinsically interconnected since the experience of redemption is the life of God in the soul. The experience of salvation through Christ is essentially a change of emotional attachment from a self-oriented pursuit of pleasure and the avoidance of pain to a new set of values, orientation, and object.

Hence, the wonder of redemption brings with it the knowledge of the character of God (an effect sharing in the nature of its cause). What is learned of God in the redemptive moment? It is that God is utterly beautiful, kind, and compassionate, that God is perfect harmony and love revealed through the infinite symmetry of all His attributes. The words of David, the 'sweet psalmist of Israel' (2 Sam 23:1), capture my thoughts:

> One thing I have asked from the LORD, that I shall seek:
> That I may dwell in the house of the LORD all the days
>   of my life,
> To behold the beauty of the LORD,
> And to meditate in His temple (Ps. 27:4).

You and I have found a friend who is not only beyond comparison with all other beings, but also One who is powerfully and deeply committed to a profound love relationship with us. Prayer is talking with the deepest of friends, the sovereign God of the universe who intimately is aware of our true needs. Prayer is the fruit of the life of God within us. To know Him is to love Him because encountering Him is to encounter infinite love; to love a person innately creates a desire for communication and that, in part, is the meaning of prayer. It is an ingredient of our responses to God, a form of listening though we may or may not verbalize them! It is old now, but forever true and eminently worth repeating; the poem, *In the Garden*, by C. Austin Miles (1868–1946) suggests the value of conversation with God in this 1912 poem that now appears in many hymnals:

> I come to the garden alone,
> While the dew is still on the roses;
> And the voice I hear, falling on my ear,
> The Son of God discloses.
>
> He speaks, and the sound of His voice
> is so sweet the birds hush their singing;
> And the melody that He gave to me
> within my heart is ringing.

Refrain:
And He walks with me, and He talks with me,
And He tells me I am His own,
And the joy we share as we tarry there,
None other has ever known.[1]

PRAYER: GOD DELIGHTS TO HEAR US

Because God is love and His activities are an expression of His character, He delights in communicating with us and receiving from us acknowledgement of that covenantal love. God's desire for His children is to bring them into greater intimacy as only vaguely pictured by the delight of parents in providing for their children and receiving the acknowledgement of their gratitude. As in the parent-child analogy, our God, our heavenly Father, is a prayer-answering God. 'He who did not spare His own Son, but delivered Him over for us all, how will He not also with Him freely give us all things?' (Rom. 8:32) As it relates to prayer, though in the context that the apostle's statement relates specifically to the believer's ground of assurance, two points can be made.

First, God is a prayer-answering God because He has made it possible to come into His presence. Not only is He the God of infinite mercy and grace, we also have a great Mediator whose sacrifice for us has atoned for our sins, purchasing the privilege of access to the Father, which Christ ensures through His priestly intercession. This access is illustrated by the rending of the curtain in the temple which separated Israelites from God. It was torn from the top to the bottom, suggestive of divine activity, so that we can enter the very throne-room presence of God (Matt. 27:51; Heb. 4:14). If God has made a provision for us to enter His presence, the

---

1. This particular hymn is found, for example, in *Great Hymns of the Faith* (Grand Rapids: Zondervan Corporation, 1974), 264.

obvious conclusion is that He desires us to do so (God cannot act in a contrary manner to Himself, though His creatures can and do!).

Second, it is a commonly repeated argument that God is not a prayer-answering God because He does not provide an answer when we ask or does not provide what was asked of Him. The answer to this complaint is, at least, threefold. Perhaps it may be that answers to our requests are not what He deemed best for us at a specific time, even though His silence may be interpreted by us as neglect or insensitivity. It may be that God has important lessons for us to learn by not removing our discomfort immediately, allowing the tears to moisten our eyes. Further, it may be that the timing is not right, and He intends to answer our prayers later on. Here the answer is simply 'not now.' We do not know the incomprehensible, infinite wisdom of God 'who works all things according to His purposes' (Rom. 8:28). We do not know why God acts in the manner that He does, but the issue of comfort in God's silences is found in the worthiness of His person to be trusted! Additionally, it may be, as Scripture often witnesses, that what we ask of God is selfish and inappropriate because it has little to do with beseeching Him so that we can praise and glorify Him more.

Prayer: A Pattern for us to Consider

One day Martin Luther decided it was time for a haircut. His barber, Peter Baskendorf, asked him a serious question that the reformer indicated he would answer, but he needed some time to reflect seriously on it. The request was this: teach me how to enter into prayer. Luther provided his answer subsequently in a little classic entitled 'A Simple Way to Pray, for a Good Friend' (1535). His prefatory comment is rather touching. 'Dear Master Peter: I will tell you as best I can what I do personally when I pray. May our dear Lord grant to you, and to everyone, to do better than I.' Luther told Peter, and perhaps even us today, that a way to prepare one's heart to enter into prayer is to use biblical passages, such as the Ten Commandments or the Lord's instructive prayer model (Matt. 6:7-15), even the Apostle's Creed, meditating on the phrases and expressing their meaning to God in prayer as preparation.

Within the historic Protestant tradition of Orthodoxy instruction in the structure of prayer is frequently explained through our Lord's comments on how to pray as recorded in Matthew 6:9ff. ('Pray, then, in this way...') The Heidelberg Catechism begins several articles on prayer (Qs. 120-29) with the question, 'What are we to pray for?' The Genevan Catechism of 1642 by John Calvin, composed to educate children, explains the meaning of our Lord's instruction answering thirty-seven questions (Qs. 258-295). Jesus instructed the disciples to pray first for the concerns and interests of God and then for our needs and interests (again, this is a model in the context of the distortions of Jesus' opponents, the Jewish religious leadership – Q. 257). This is a wonderful model structurally for our prayer life though we may want to add a third category, prayer for the needs of others.

Prayer: Some Concluding Thoughts

As we draw this chapter to its conclusion it seems fitting to reflect on a few practical matters. It is important to remember that we all have our strengths and weaknesses when it comes to the disciplines of the spiritual life. For all of us, one or another of the things we discuss may prove really hard (you cannot remove personality from spirituality!). Remember, the issue is the development of habits. Habits are often arduous in the developmental stages, but with persistence they become a delight. Let me say a few things in somewhat of a list-fashion.

First, the posture of prayer is not important; it is our attitudes and earnestness that is crucial. In the Scriptures you will find the posture of kneeling, but also of standing; some are seen praying with closed eyes, yet there are other instances of eyes lifted toward heaven. Sometimes hands are clasped together while there are instances of outstretched arms and hands. Some have told me that they find praying while walking to be most productive for them.

Second, the location of prayer is not regulated in the Bible. Jonah, of course, prayed in rather unpleasant, even horrifying, circumstances; Jesus often prayed in secluded places, such as a garden. John Wesley, the eighteenth-century revivalist preacher, took Matthew 6:6 literally and had a private prayer closet. The issue is that we should find a location and manner that fits where we are in life.

Third, the length of our prayer is not of upmost importance. The issue in our approach to the throne of grace is that of spiritual integrity, affection, and faith, not the number of words we choose. Clearly, prayer is not an attempt to exhort benefit from a reluctant God or to inform and instruct Him. Some of the great prayers in the Bible are brief, whereas others are lengthy, and often they are determined by circumstance.

Fourth, some people find it hard to pray alone, others find it difficult to pray in a group. As a general rule, if anyone finds a task too difficult, they will discontinue it or ameliorate the pain somewhat. If you find it hard to pray, you might find it helpful to join a group and simply listen to the petitions of others, so entering with them in prayer.

As a teenager, I had a unique experience with group-prayer that has deeply shaped my life. I was then attending a small, traditional Baptist church. What I found most fascinating was the attendance at their Wednesday evening prayer meeting. It was quite well attended; however, what amazed me was the earnestness of those who prayed. I can truly say that listening to the prayers, and particularly the manner of their praying, has shaped me and my understanding of prayer to this day. Those dear folks, their lives now a faded memory for the most part, gave me a treasure. Praying in a group, listening to prayers, strengthened my faith, making me grateful. Sadly, many of our churches have abandoned the corporate weekly prayer meeting.

Fifth, a simple way to help you to pray with more regularity is to construct a prayer list that you can carry about in a pocket, say on a 3x5 card. If you are married, I would suggest that you and your mate make a list and hold each other accountable to pray together. A list will simply jog your memory and when answers arrive you have a vivid reminder that God is a prayer-answering God.

Sixth, spend time with people listening to their stories and what is important in their lives whether it be family members, friends, or co-workers. Knowing the heart-wrenching needs of others not only draws us closer to them but invigorates our prayers for them and shapes our witness to them. We live in a broken world and the brokenness of it should cause us to turn to God who alone is the answer!!

QUESTIONS FOR DISCUSSION

1. How has this discussion on prayer helped you?

2. What do you find are the greatest hindrances to a regular time of prayer, whatever the length, every day?

3. If prayer is far more than asking, what is it?

4. While the chapter has addressed some ways to facilitate prayer, have you found others in your walk with God?

5. What are the most personal prayer needs that you have, that your immediate family have, that a friend has, and that a co-worker has? Is this not the substance of a prayer list?

11

Right Thoughts Require Good Input:
The Benefit of Community

Thoughts entertained become acts pursued. The spiritual life takes place in the context of adversaries of all that is right and wholesome, a blighted world of alluring attractions, yet false values; our twisted human nature that, at times, if not often, seeks comfort, pleasure, and adjudication over care and compassion toward others; and a powerful adversary that seeks our destruction and the failure of God's earthly kingdom (Eph. 2:2-4; 6:12; 1 Pet. 5:8-9). Further, the experience of walking with God is controlled by the kind of information we entertain mentally since thoughts lead to choices, and choices lead to actions. When the mind is set on heavenly things, our lives reflect the character of heaven (Rom. 8:6-7; Col. 3:1-2)!

The topic in this section of the book is this: How do we find and cultivate good thoughts because good input leads to good outcomes, just as erroneous, destructive information, when approved and not dismissed, leads to regrettable outcomes? We are in the process of enumerating several sources of good thoughts with which we can fill our minds (and we will continue to do so below). However, it is time to state a few caveats and remove a few possible misperceptions.

First, the means of acquiring good ideas (e.g., Bible reading, prayer, meditation) are not lineal, sequential steps in a mechanical process of accomplishment. That is, it is not about doing one until you are comfortable and then adding another until the list is completed. What is being described is a circle containing interrelated activities that are to be approached simultaneously.

Second, and alluded to above, the several disciplines overlap; they are to be pursued together and interconnected with regularity. It is a process, not an accomplishment! As we read the Bible we are to think on what we are reading (that is called meditation); when we pray, we are to do so through the lens of our reading with meditation.

Third, we should not despair in our struggles with the multi-tasking endeavor of incorporating the disciplines of a walk with God. Remember when you were learning to ride a bicycle, sitting on the seat and then putting both feet on the pedals was not easy. Then attempting to push them without falling off in the process was daunting, not to mention doing so while keeping our hands on the handlebars. What we had to master was multi-tasking and balancing while avoiding immoveable objects like trees and cars. Then we had to grapple with speed and manoeuvring issues. It only came through trial and error, but one day we did it. Difficulties were dissolved and things became a routine (I will not get into the art of driving a car, but I trust you get what I am suggesting).

THE IMPORTANCE OF PUBLIC WORSHIP
Observers of the American expression of Christian faith have indicated that it emphasizes the individual often to the neglect of its corporate aspects, that we are part of the body of Christ, a singularity composed of a plurality. Perhaps this can be attributed to the uniqueness of our

social and cultural national experience, perhaps also the radical commercialization of values. While the Bible often speaks of individual believers, frequently it sees believers acting together as a spiritual unity (the Scriptures refer to us as a collectivity called 'saints,' but it does not use the term for individual believers). All of this suggests that growth toward increased spiritual maturity is hindered when the emphasis is only placed on the private aspects alone (we have emphasized the importance of group prayer above). Simply put, there are corporate aspects to growth that are as important as the individualized ones.

Priority in the Holy Scriptures is placed upon the regular assembly of God's people; by tradition the norm quickly became the first day of the week (Acts 20:7; 1 Cor 16:2). The central focus for the gathering of God's people is worship expressed in the proclamation of the Word of God and the observance of the sacraments, baptism being an outward symbol of entrance into the family of God, and thus not repeatable, and the Lord's Table being symbolic of the fellowship the Christian enjoys having been engrafted into Christ.

The point in regard to our topic is that regular attendance for the hearing of God's Word in the corporate context is imperative. Not only should we gather to hear the preaching of God's Word, but the educational study programmes of the church are important for the spiritual health of all age groups. The writer to the Hebrews spoke of the gathering of believers in this way: 'let us consider how to stimulate one another to love and good deeds, not forsaking our own assembling together as is the habit of some, but encouraging one another' (Heb. 10:24-25). Listening, as well as social interaction in a class-like format, is a grand source of positive input.

While we have emphasized the importance of hearing God's Word through gifted pastor-preachers in a formal setting accompanied with singing, prayers, and testimony, which in most instances is unilateral, being confined to listening as opposed to active participation and dialogue, participating in the educational programs of the church, as well as being involved in a small fellowship, are a rich source of positive, strengthening input. The sharing of needs leading to engagement in prayer and the potential for healthy and inspiring social conversation has the potentially of truly being significant.

Another corporate activity within the context of the church that promotes good ideas through healthy input is regular participation in the Lord's Table which frequently is denominated by the words sacrament (meaning a mystery) or ordinance (meaning a rule or prescription). As such, the religious ceremony has a twofold function according to the Westminster Larger Catechism (Q 162): First, the elements signify something far greater than themselves, the bread symbolizes the true giver and sustainer of life and the cup His sacrificial death, our life springing out of His death. Second, holding and partaking of them is a seal, an attestation, of God's good pleasure toward us. The value of the Table is that we are called regularly to remember the very cause of our faith, the cost of our faith, and the necessity of witnessing to our faith. A term used frequently of the Table is Eucharist; the word means 'thanksgiving', a refreshing moment of individual and collective intimacy with our Redeemer. Hearing the Word of God and participating in the Table of the Lord with its symbolism are the greatest occasions of worship by the believer (Matt. 26:26-28; 1 Cor. 11:23-25).

In speaking of the role of church participation as an important source of constructive input, allow me to pause and say something as to the importance of setting aside a special day in the cycle of the week as a day reserved for rest from the routines that characterize the other six. For most of us, that day is reserved for Sunday, the Lord's Day. That it is to be a day for private and corporate worship has been previously cited, yet here I mean more than that. The 'sabbath' is to be a day of setting aside the normal activities associated with gainful employment, but it is also a time for rest and to show mercy and kindness to those in special need. While pursuit of work is commendable, and earning a living a necessity, a day set aside for special religious activities, a day of ceasing activities and trusting God to provide for us, is important for our spiritual development.

Another profitable source of good ideas is found in reading wholesome literature. Quality devotional literature, what we call Christian Classics, have become increasingly available since the invention of the printing press, introduced in the West through Johannes of Gutenberg in the fifteenth century. Augmenting, even eclipsing print-material, is digital material. Books are now available to us in a variety of audio formats. DVDs and CDs are readily accessed by the busy traveler. Instead of allowing our minds to simply wander aimlessly, normally giving way to our fears or earthly desires, why not listen to an audio book or sermon as you traverse to and from your workplace?

THE IMPORTANCE OF GOOD COMPANY

'Bad company corrupts good morals' is an age-old moral adage, often repeated as though it was something out of Benjamin Franklin's wit and wisdom. Actually, it is found in the Scriptures (1 Cor. 15:33); it is timeless and true. Good ideas, healthy thoughts, come from being around good people. James, the blunt preacher, said it this way, 'Does a fountain send out from the same opening both fresh and bitter water? Can a fig tree, my brethren, produce olives, or a vine produce figs? Neither can salt water produce fresh' (James 3:11-12). If our advice givers are unwise and incompetent, their instruction will partake of its source, just as it is true in James' appeal to nature. People are more convoluted than the natural world in some respects.

We must all be careful and concerned about whom we listen to, though I am not suggesting that we should only seek advice from believers since wisdom and knowledge is not solely to be found there. We have had very helpful people in our lives who proved to be caring and insightful even though they were not Christ-followers; wisdom is not the sole privilege of the redeemed. However, spiritual counsel, advice being of its nature spiritual, is to be found among believers (in acquiring wisdom relative to purchasing a vehicle, the need for a particular surgery, or the handling of a legal issue, we may be better left to competent unbelievers than those who are believers, but who lack training or insight in those fields).

With the above caveat, in the realm of helping others in their walk with the Lord, it is best to consult those who know Him; input is important in spiritual growth. Allow me to offer a few suggestions.

First, being by nature relational, communicative beings, though admittedly marred by the blight of human sin, excessive isolationism and reclusiveness is a barrier to spiritual health and growth. It is integral that we all participate socially with like-minded people who care for us as we care for them, people with whom we can share our deepest thoughts and fears without fear of recrimination or gossiping. Our deepest needs are not to be found in intellectual content alone, but also in relationships characterized by openness, care, and forgiveness. Make a sincere effort to cultivate a small circle of friends with whom you can enjoy serious, wholesome conversation, enjoying mutual interests together such as athletic events, concerts, or a movie.

Knowing that the issue of close friends is much harder for the male species to engage in than females, that men tend to be self-protectionist and less open to share their fears and frustrations (older men, retirees, do not find this so acute seeing the need for comraderies [hence the daily visit to the coffee shop]), it is simply worth the risk of self-disclosure. For several years I was in a group of three other men, Christians. Once a month one of us would choose a movie on a rotating basis, meet for dinner at a local restaurant, and after the movie go to a coffee shop to discuss what we saw. One of the fellows was a white-collar business professional, another mowed the lawn in a cemetery (he once told us that his job was executive, having countless hundreds under him), another was a paper hanger and painter, and I a clergyman and theological professor. Though very diverse, we shared our Lord together and our friendships became deeply meaningful and mutually beneficial. We all need friends, and what can be greater than friends who love the Lord!

The Importance of Wholesome Activities
When two of Jesus' disciples sought a supreme place of honor in our Lord's kingdom (Matt. 20:20-21), Jesus explained to them that seeking acceptance through prominence, as opposed to servitude, is not the way to greatness for a Christ-follower. In the world, push and shove characterizes those who are led to believe that the quest for prominence, position, and titles is the path to

human significance. Jesus' point is diametrically opposite; significance in His kingdom is found in accepting our insignificance while using our gifts, talents, and privileges in the service of others, for the profit of others, and not for ourselves. Emphatically, Jesus declared, 'It is not so among you, but whoever wishes to be great among you shall be your servant... just as the Son of Man did not come to be served but to serve and give His life a ransom for many' (Matt. 20:26, 28).

Growing spiritually is not simply a matter of the individual development of certain routines and habits. Input is a necessity, yet there is something more; there must be output. We grow as we dispense the use of our time and talents in the service of others. There is simply more to spiritual maturity than reading the Bible, praying, and gatherings for fellowship and mutual edification. An indispensable ingredient in spiritual maturity is service, for it is in giving of ourselves that we receive. Consistent with the thesis of these chapters, good thoughts, thoughts of God and His purposes in the world, are a product of good input. A component of good input is service to others. We grow as we exert; as we give out, we are given.

Fear is a repeated motivation for inactivity as is the claim of encumbrance by a variety of duties and pressing circumstances (are we all not busy people?). Another common argument for spiritual inertia is a lack of spiritual giftedness. The emptiness of such arguments, and many others, is that God is the One who alone accounts for anyone's productivity. What I have learned through decades of observation is that God uses those who make themselves available to Him, not the most talented but simply the available. Moses offered a classic excuse when God called him to lead His people. He replied that he was not articulate in speech. How could he energize and create loyalty for a greater cause with speech deficiencies? The Lord's answer to Moses was twofold: first, He has made no mistakes in the manner of His creating us (Exod. 4:11) and, second, our effectiveness for Him is not rooted in our talents, but in the promises of His presence before us and with us (Exod. 4:12). You will never know the depth of God's willingness to use you until you set out in faith and adventure.

Years ago I accompanied a group of high schoolers on a camping trip into the mountains of Arkansas. While things generally went well, a personal crisis came when, in the midst of watching the young people enthusiastically enjoying rock-rappelling, I was asked to join them. Standing with my back to the cliff, grasping the rope and firmly secured in the harness, a young man clasped the rope on one end and I the other. Fear gripped me when he said to me, 'Lean back.' I replied, 'Will this rope hold?' The teenager's reply has not left my mind for decades. He said, 'Sir, you will never know until you lean back.' The same is true in the service of the Lord through the service of others. When we trust, when we lean back, then we will discover the strength of the 'rope.'

I am convinced that it is not talent that makes for a successful life in the service of the Lord. The most important ingredient in overcoming our fears of venturing out is love, a love for God and a love for people. What you cherish most is what motivates. If fear motivates, then withdrawal is our natural tendency; if the love of God for us motivates, we will naturally express that emotion in caring for His children. The second most important ingredient in overcoming our fears of rejection is simply taking the time to see the enormous needs around us. Because of a willingness to see need for the sake of the Savior, His love will cast out the predominance of our reticence.

How can this be applied? What can you and I consider doing if service for God by serving others is a conduit to good thoughts? Have you considered assisting in the children's or adult education programme at your church? Are their special outreach activities sponsored by your church that you can assist? Have you considered a short-term mission trip? Are their widows in the church who you could fix things for about their homes or their cars (take it to a car wash, have the car inspected, assist in getting the car to a repair shop, help with errands)? Are there single parents in your church who need time alone on a Saturday morning and you could take their children to a park and a treat for an hour or two? The power to execute a thank-you-note is often a small endeavor, but the result can be deeply encouraging.

While these are only samples of the options that are available to investigate, talent is really not the issue; it is willingness to give up the non-renewable resource of time, a willingness to take the time to see what is about you. When we see with a believing heart of love, we all engage, but it requires time spent in seeing.

As we close this section of the book, which has been a discussion of the positive endeavors that accrue to our spiritual progress and the sources of constructive input, the assumption underlying these chapters is that good input fosters good outcomes, that good thoughts pondered will result in good decisions, and that good decisions lead to beneficial actions. While more is yet to be considered, I want to end with a few reminders.

First, spiritual growth is a process; it is not accomplished at a meeting or in a single resolve. Remember, a tree grows imperceivably over time, yet it can become majestic. The spiritual life is a marathon, not a sprint. We should endeavor to do what we can rather than too much.

Second, none of us can do all the things listed above at the same time. Choose small goals in your spiritual development strategy, but then work on consistency. Remember the goal is progress, not perfection. Perfection is the hobgoblin of small, diluted minds (more about that later).

Third, when you stop doing what you know is right, you should start over again! The chief characteristic of the saint's life is not how well we are doing but what we do when we are not doing well.

Fourth, the Lord is more interested in the development of our lives as spiritual mirrors than we are. Therefore, He brings things into our lives, both of negative and positive events, to shape and mold us. Pain and disappointments are wonderful surgical tools in the hands of an infinitely wise, all-powerful, and deeply loving Friend (Gen. 49:20; Exod. 3:10; Judg. 6:3).

QUESTIONS FOR DISCUSSION

1. As you reflect on the topics in the chapter, what are your general thoughts?

2. If the Lord's Table is an integral component of worship, and somewhat under-emphasized in many churches, what do you think can be done to stress its importance?

3. Would you add fasting to the list of spiritual disciplines?

4. What is being done and what can be done in our churches to get greater participation in the daily outreach so as to facilitate greater spiritual maturity?

5. Can you think of things you could be doing through your church and in your neighbourhood that they are not doing as a way to serve and honor Christ?

6. Can you think of experiences in your life when you were glad you overcame your fears and reached out of your comfort zone to help people? Why are you thankful that you did so? What lessons did you learn?

SECTION 4

NEGATIVE ACTIONS THAT ENHANCE POSITIVE SPIRITUAL GROWTH

Thus far the discussion of the spiritual life has comprised two general foci: first, we began with an emphasis upon understanding what God has done and is doing daily in and for us that makes spiritual growth, a maturing in Christlikeness, a possibility. These and other matters, including certain qualifications, are found in the first two sections of the book. Section 3 turned from background, presuppositional insights to a delineation of the positive ingredients, called the spiritual disciplines, the things we can do that promote the development of healthy ideas (obviously, healthy ideas are a fruit of accessing healthy sources of information, and healthy ideas lead to healthy choices and consequent behavioral patterns).

In this section, the emphasis in its chapters shifts from positive input to the removal of negative behavioral patterns, many leftover coping mechanisms developed from early childhood and perfected in the context of more sophisticated contexts, such as peer-group relationships, marriage, the work environment, or general socializing. The summarizing verse for what will be explained subsequently is Romans 8:13: '… if you are living according to the flesh you must die, but if you by the Spirit are putting to death the deeds of the flesh, you will live.' Paul was writing to a church with interpersonal struggles, a failure to get along with fellow believers, and he subsequently wrote, 'Therefore accept one another, just as Christ has also accepted us to the glory of God' (Rom. 15:7). At least one scholar makes the claim that this is the apostle's central concern in the book. It is little wonder that Paul would give instruction concerning this important subject.

The question before us is this, how do we go about putting to death the 'deeds of the flesh,' thoughts and actions inconsistent with emulating the character of Jesus as a Christ-follower? How can you and I remove the inconsistencies in our walk with God that are nothing short of its proper definition, sin? It is a life-long endeavor for reasons that will be disclosed subsequently.

12

GOOD NEWS AND BAD NEWS:

WHY THE STRUGGLE WITH SIN PERSISTS IN THOSE RESCUED FROM ITS CONDEMNING POWER

Most of us will have heard a stirring conference speaker or a caring pastor who left us in a state of angst or bewilderment by presenting to us as a non-negotiable reality what seemed so contrary to our Christian experience. We heard that our identity with Christ through the regenerating work of the Spirit of God has resulted in our death to sin, that the necessity of sinfulness has ended through a baptism into His death. We were reminded of the words of Paul in the Book of Romans such as 'How shall we who died to sin live in it any longer?' (6:2) or 'for he who has died has been freed from sin' (6:7). The emphasis seems unmistakable in the apostle; a death has occurred: 'Death no longer has dominion over you' (6:9b). The result of this death is that the grip of sin has been broken: 'For sin shall not be master over you for you are not under law but grace' (6:14).

Initially, such an emphasis presents us with a dilemma; it seems contrary to daily experience. It takes little personal reflection to recognize it. For example, if we had a screen on our foreheads that revealed our inner thoughts and motivations for others to see, I think we would have less friends and far more controversy! A confident, assertive demeanor may only be a facade to mask our uncertainties and fears; the appearance of humility may disguise deep insecurities, a paranoid-like dread of possible rejection by our peers. Simply put, expressions of piety are often subterfuges for self-gain! Has not every husband at one time or another showed kindness and tenderness to obtain an intimacy with a mate? Has not every wife laid aside legitimate feelings to prevent being demeaned and rejected by the one she loves? Have not ladies conceded their moral ideals out of fear of losing what might lead to a successful and desired union in marriage? Have we all not shaded our consciences to please our employer so to appear loyal and secure advancement? How many times have we fumed when drivers did not observe traffic lane rules and cut into the line resulting in thoughts that should not be verbalized? Hasn't Jesus told us that after loving God, we must love our brother or sister, human kindness being the whole point of the Law (Matt. 22:37-40)? Did not the apostle John make this abundantly clear in 1 John 4:23-24? The scenarios are endless! The point is simply that there seems to be a disjuncture between what the apostle writes and our daily Christian experience. Why would Paul tell us, 'Consider yourselves to be dead to sin' (Rom. 6:11), if we are dead-dead?

This dilemma is not only true to experience; it is clearly revealed in Holy Scripture. In chapter seven of Romans, Paul makes this remarkable statement: 'I find then a principle that evil is present in me, the one who wishes to do good' (7:21). The tense of the verbs in this paragraph (vv. 14-25) are present tense, suggesting an enduring reality in the apostle's post-conversion experience. The 'I' in this passage is one who 'delights in God's law' (v. 22), seeks to obey it (vv. 15-20), and 'serve' it (v. 25); in 7:22 and 25 we are told that this 'I' serves the law of God through the mind. The unbeliever is described as hostile to God (1:28), he does not seek after God (3:11), and simply cannot submit to the law of God (8:7). Paul had a transformation, a death, but it did not leave him devoid of struggles!

Without the use of Romans 7:14-25, since some scholars are not agreed that the passage speaks of Paul in his regenerate state, the Bible elsewhere is explicit in the assertion that all believers will struggle with sin as an ever-present reality in their lives. If it were not the case, why do we have dire warnings to desist from certain actions, numerous commands to discontinue particular practices, and the variegated examples of sinning saints to avoid? Why are we told to confess our sins and of certain remedies when we do, if we have undergone a death (1 John 1:5–2:2)? Why are we informed, '... if we judge ourselves, we should not be judged' (1 Cor. 11:31)?

Thus, we are faced with what appears to be a dilemma, a challenge. How do we resolve this? Where do we begin? First, what I know is that God, being infinite wisdom and knowledge, is incapable of confusion or being confused; it is simply contrary to His character, His uprightness and integrity being the foundation out of which flows all His actions, including communication.

Second, just as disclosure to us of His character is unconfused and unsullied through the incarnate person of the Son of God, the Lord Jesus Christ (Heb. 1:1-4), so it is with the written description of Himself that we find in the Holy Scriptures, the work of God through human authors being a work of divine superintendence. The unity of the living Word and the written Word is, thus, guaranteed through the ministry of the Spirit of God through people who have described for us the activities of the Father and the Son resulting in our salvation. The answer to our dilemma is found in carefully defining and nuancing terms!

What Does it Mean that we have Died to Sin?

Simply put, we have died to the universal, unrelenting grip of sin over every faculty of our immaterial being (our minds, our conscience, our affections, and our wills), but not its presence in our lives and its residual effect, should we grant consent to it. You and I have suffered a wonderful transformation from an abject, irremediable state of unwillingness to obey God, a dire state of rebellion against Him (Rom. 1:24, 26, 28; Eph. 4:17; Col. 2:18), to having a renewed mind, conscience, affections, and will. 'Things I loved before have passed away and things I love far more have come to stay', states an oft-repeated line, but not all things of old have done so! That awaits our final redemption, a deliverance that is now only in progress.

There are several implications which flow from the insight that the willingness to sin is not what we had 'died to,' but it is in the sphere of its universality, the unmitigated and unrelenting death-grip that is gone forever.

First, this means that the 'normal' Christian is characterized by struggle, a struggle to be willing to do what God says, even though inner urges and outward solicitations raise serious questions as to its propriety. The normal Christian life is not about reaching some beatific plateau wherein our struggles end, but indeed one wherein new struggles are discovered.

Second, while we all struggle in some respects, we do not all struggle in the same areas. This means that we can help each other. We are all fellow strugglers seeking to increasingly bring 'what we shall be' (1 John 3:2) into the 'now' of our experience. No one is above being helped, nor is any believer unable to help another struggler.

Third, it means that there is no reason to hide our 'secrets,' thinking that those you trust will think less of you. Of course, care in the extent, manner, and circumstance of disclosure must be cautiously pursued, even within a culture of trust, for some do twist confidences and leverage gossip. Having a fellow traveler who can offer wise, seasoned advice is of great value.

How do we Know that we have Died to Sin?

If the struggle with sin is a reality for us who have died to sin through the provision of Christ and forgiveness, and the consequent indwelling of the Spirit is the divine life of God within each of us, how can we know that our struggles are post-death ones and that we indeed are possessors of the life of God? We all carry a guilty conscience and we all have moral failures, called sins of commission and omission, so how can we distinguish the actions of unbelievers from true believers when the presence of sin is found in all of us as revealed by our failures and actions?

First, what distinguishes the sin of one who has suffered a spiritual eclipse, what Paul calls 'death to sin,' is that such a failure is not the fruit of perpetual rebellion; it is not about the continuance of actions that becomes a remorseless habit, even an occasion for boasting, or an abounding principle in our lives.[1] Let me propose an illustration; it has to do with a pencil, a sheet of paper,

---

1. I am aware of the sin-unto-death-passage in 1 Corinthians 11:27-28, but I take it to mean that believers can be so dominated by sin that their witness for Christ is wasted and they no longer appreciate God's wisdom and act to the contrary, repudiating His kindness, and become a hindrance to His kingdom-work on earth. In such a case, out of love and benevolence, He may take them to be with Himself ('saved so as by fire,' 1 Cor. 3:15) by sanctioning what appears to have been fatal tragedy. To believers, the writer to the Hebrews writes, 'It is a terrifying thing to fall into the hands of the living God' (Heb. 10:31).

and etching dots on the page with the pencil. All people are sinners, even those who have been allowed to know the God of the universe in a redemptive manner. On the 'page' of all of our lives are those dots, some larger than others. The difference between those of a believer and a non-believer is that the former's dots are scattered about and not so frequently practiced. Those sins are not habitual to such a degree that they describe the lives of believers. For them, 'death' has not erased the dots, but it has greatly curtailed them, creating space between them on our page!

Second, we know that the dominion of sin has been crushed because God has created in us a willingness to be willing, to see the sins in our lives for the value that God places upon them. When we were without the life of God, it was the fear of loss and the hope of advantage that curbed our lusts and inordinate appetites; it was the love of self that brought the pangs of conscience, that little voice within, the mere remnants of a once heightened barometer of right and wrong. Our 'little voice within' has been re-oriented; it is not the fear of loss that now motivates our behavior; now it is fear of dishonoring the One who loved us and purchased us by His own precious blood. Simply put, we are people who may be slow to heed warnings, violating our own convictions, but we intuitively know that God is right and anything contrary is indefensible. We are not those who have contempt for and despise the ways of God; we are just rebellious little children!

Third, we now know that we should do certain things and not treat them as trivialities, despising or abandoning the means that God has provided for us as sources for spiritual nourishment and consequent growth. Regular attendance in the assembly of Christian people is not an option; God has singularly ordained the church, the gathering where through Word and sacrament we hear and rehearse through symbolism and thoughtful meditation the wonders of our divine redemption. While arguments can be offered in criticism of the church, it is without doubt integral, and all believers should feel an emptiness when not availing themselves of what it affords: spiritual grace, fellowship, consolation, correction, and exhortation. Hearing the Word in whatever form (a Bible study, a worship service, educational programmes, fellowship gatherings to share and care) are attractive to us when at one time they would have held no value or we attended them only through any variety of external stimuli (parental insistence, to see our friends, to be accepted into a group, to date a hopeful).

Fourth, evidence that we have undergone the inception of death to sin is not that we do not continue in old behaviors, and even develop new, negative ones on occasion; it is that we accept correction from those who see our delinquencies and care enough about us to confront us. When we are thus reproofed by a friend, mate, or colleague, we do not seek to defend it with all manner of creative excuses, passive-aggressive reactions (conceding to it, yet blaming others for our derelictions and not taking personal responsibility [the old line, 'The devil made me do it']). The Bible teaches that while solicitation may be external or environmental, concession is a personal, voluntary choice every time. You know that some kind of 'death' has happened when you see your choices as your personal responsibility, your failure as an affront to the almighty, faithful God of heaven and earth, and repent of your sins. The truly redeemed people have a new set of priorities created by a new set of values. The mark of the saint is not only determined by how well he is doing; it is also determined by what he does when he is not doing well! When we see things as the holy God does, we know that a 'death' has occurred! When what we engage in leads to the wounding of our God and Savior, Jesus Christ, then we know a 'death' has overtaken us!

An Appropriate Illustration: A Flight over a 'Forest'

Let me illustrate the idea of our death to sin with the use of a metaphor. Imagine that you are in a commercial aircraft ascending above 10,000 feet or descending below that height. As you look out of your passenger window, seeing a forest below, how can the forest explain what it means to have 'died' to sin?

The day before you came to embrace the Savior, if you looked out the airplane window upon the ground below, you would see a forest, a forest that symbolizes your life. What would you see? You would see a dense, unmitigating, unbroken blanket of trees, weeds, and vines. That is the state and condition of every person who is unwilling to recognize their lostness and flee for refuge to Christ.

Let us suppose that you did come to embrace the Redeemer of all mankind and you were again at ten thousand feet above the earth. Looking down on the 'forest' below, representing your new life in Christ, what would you see? What difference did redemption make in the forest of your life, even though you would be only days old in the faith? There would still be trees, weeds, and encroaching vines; however, you would see something else, something rather remarkable. You would also see clearings in the landscape. Some of the trees, weeds and vines would have been uprooted, though some of all three varieties remain in the 'forest' of our lives. This is the difference in the landscape of an unbeliever's life and struggles and that of a believer!

Questions for Discussion

1. How has the discussion of the cause of our struggle with sin encouraged you in your struggles?

2. In what way in your life can you see that trees, weeds, and vines have been uprooted in the 'forest' of your life?

3. What one big tree would you like to see cut down in your 'forest'?

4. Is it a comfort to you to know that you do not have to have sinful reactions, attitudes, and actions? If sin is voluntary, a matter of personal willingness or unwillingness, for the believer, how does it help you make choices?

5. Is there a particular tree, weed, or vine in your relationship to someone else that you would like to see removed from the 'forest' of your life?

6. What advantages have come to your spiritual life since the dominion of sin has been broken asunder by the intrusion of the grace of God? How have you changed? Did your best friend notice a change?

13

THE SOURCE OF THE BELIEVER'S STRUGGLE:
A YET-TO-BE-COMPLETED REDEMPTION

The redemptive mercies of Christ are inexplicably profound and astoundingly wonderful. We have entered into a new family, the family of God. The Bible makes this abundantly evident. Paul writes, for example, to the Colossian believers: 'He has delivered us from the domain of darkness and translated [transferred] us into the kingdom of his beloved Son, in whom we have redemption, the forgiveness of sins' (1:13-14). Elsewhere he asserts that God 'made us alive together with Christ (by grace you have been saved) and raised us up with him and seated us with him in the heavenly places in Christ Jesus' (Eph. 2:5-6). The point of the apostle's comments, and numerous others by him as well, is that we have been brought into a new status; we have been placed 'in Christ.'

As stated in the previous chapter, we have suffered a death when we came to life through the divine mercies of God by the grace of Christ through the Spirit. We have died to the universal, unrelenting grip of involuntary enslavement to sin, to the fruit of living solely in the domain of darkness. We have been forgiven and, with divine acquittal, have been robed in the righteousness of Christ and made citizens of a new world, far more expansive and beautiful, than the one we once thought was everything.

With all of that being true, what can we say about the struggles that all of us have as believers with the values and priorities that remain with us from the darkness of our former citizenship? Why do we so identify with Paul's insight into his own interior spiritual life when he writes, 'I find, then, the principle that evil is present in me, the one who wishes to do good. For I joyfully concur with the law of God, in the inner man, but I see a different law in the members of my body, waging war against the law of my mind, and making me a prisoner of the law of sin which is in my members. Wretched man that I am! Who will set me free from this body of death? Thanks be to God through Jesus Christ our Lord! So then, I myself with my mind am serving the law of God with my mind, but on the other, with my flesh, I serve the law of sin' (Rom. 7:21-25).

There is a reason that you and I can so identify with Paul in the above passage. While we have died to sin's condemning power, we have not, as yet, been delivered from its presence. Indeed, we find ourselves in allegiance to 'two kingdoms'; a kingdom whose grip we are passing from and a kingdom that we have only begun to enter in Christ. Sin's universal condemning grasp has been broken, but its presence is only gradually being retired. Such dual citizenry explains the dark sides of all our lives: our lack of trust in God and willingness to believe that our inventions are superior to God's directives, that our anger is allowed, that our broken promises are not sinful (the list is endless)!

The Reality of Sin's Presence: Indwelling Sin

While the Bible is clear that the darkness of sin's condemning power has been forever crushed by the infusion of grace that emanates from Calvary, we all have our struggles. If I am now in the 'Kingdom of Light,' why do I find temporal solace in the 'Kingdom of Darkness'? Simply put, a massive deliverance has happened, but it will not be experientially completed until the day we pass from our attachment to our dark citizenry when we pass into a new realm of existence; it is assured, but it simply has not arrived yet!

It seems that this can be argued in several ways. First, the Bible is replete with instructions, commands, and illustrations suggestive of sin's presence in the believer's life. For example, Paul's instructions in Romans 6 only make sense if believers struggle with the continuance of sin: 'Consider yourselves to be dead to sin' (6:11); 'Do not let sin reign in your mortal body, that you should obey its lusts' (6:12); 'Do not go on presenting the members of your body to sin as instruments of unrighteousness, but present yourselves to God as those alive from the dead' (6:13). The present tense of the commands in these passages, and many others, suggests a negative reality that should grieve us who seek to walk in the light, having been transformed by the gospel.

Second, the Bible abounds with negative examples of the sinful actions of believers. The inappropriate behavior of Corinthian believers at the Lord's Table brought a severe reprimand from the apostle (1 Cor. 11:17-22) and a dire reality (1 Cor. 11:27-32). The 'sweet psalmist of Israel,' the godly David, was not above the sin of trusting in his own military establishment rather than having confidence in God (2 Sam. 24:10), though we know also of his travesty with Bathsheba, the murder of Uriah, and the tragic aftermath (2 Sam. 11–12). Moses, in disobedience, struck the rock in anger (Num. 20:11). The greed of Ananias and the complicity of his wife illumines the reality of a twistedness of soul, even in believers (Acts 5:1-11). The heartless departure of some of the churches in Revelation 2–3 is but a microcosm of the collectivity of redeemed individuality.

Third, our personal experiences are clear evidence that we all are victimized by our own wilful ignorance, improper delights, purposeful misperceptions, and calculated rebellions. For example, is it not uncommon to suppose that sin is not so bad if we can find a greater abundance of love, kindness, and obedience in our lives? Why do we rationalize evil by excusing a little of it in our lives? Why is it that we can choose to live in avoidance of the major cultural and ecclesiastical sins, while allowing ourselves to be entertained by the private lusts of the heart? Is that true godliness? Why is it that we more often are attracted to bad examples of conduct than to good examples? Why do we think thoughts in private that we would be embarrassed about if they should be revealed?

THE OCCASIONS OF SIN'S MANIFESTATION WITHIN US

The presence of distorted affections toward God and nonconformity to the directives of the Holy Scriptures are experiential realities, truths that are so rooted in our common experience that observation is sufficient to prove the assertion; that is, when we analyze the patterns of our behavior the evidence is irrefutable. While we have been delivered from the condemning power of sin, God's wrath assuaged through the death of death in the death of Christ for us, the presence of sin continues. The twistedness of our present condition is extensive, reaching to every faculty of our immaterial being (the mind, emotions, affections, and will), a reality designated by the term 'flesh' in the Bible. As such, it is beneficial for our subsequent discussions to pause and reflect on how the remaining power of sin operates in our lives. Allow me to elucidate a few ideas.

First, have you not noticed that failure to avail yourself of the disciplined regularity of spiritual input (thinking about God intentionally, reading the Bible, prayer, worship) leads to actions and thoughts contrary to the character of God? Neglect never leads to improvement in any realm of our lives. When input is neglected, input does not cease. It simply opens the opportunity to receive input of another sort. It fuels our own destructive, our yet-to-be-redeemed choices and behaviors.

Second, indwelling sin, the remnants of sin's once universal control of our lives, always becomes manifest when we simultaneously lose our fear of God. Have you noticed that when you fill your mind with the things of God, viewing Him as altogether beautiful and desirable, that sin does not crouch at our door? Have you noticed that every time we sin, the simultaneous circumstance is unbelief in the goodness of God and the worthiness of His instructions? Every time we sin, we do so by first convincing ourselves that our thoughts are better than God's, that we know better what is best for us than God does, that God has designed the Christian life so as to make us only somewhat fulfilled and we need to figure out how to improve on His ways with us. Simply stated, you and I lack trust in the goodness of God, and its manifestation is in thinking that our contrivances are superior to God's ways. Our minds are subject to deception!

Third, indwelling sin is manifest also in our failure to understand that Satan is far more than a fellow marching about in a red outfit with long ears and a protruding tail carrying a pitchfork. He is the archenemy of our souls (1 Pet. 5:8), the father of lies (John 8:44). The devil and his minions are master psychologists having insight into your particular weaknesses of character, the yet-unredeemed dark rooms of your soul. He tailors his poisoned arrows for the places you are most subject to attack. The Bible tells us pointedly that we are to resist (1 Pet. 5:9; James 4:7) his encroachments, deceiving us with false promises and allurements that appeal to the remnants of sin's once total sway over our souls, saying, 'Follow me!'

Fourth, one of the chief ways that sin manifests itself in our lives is the errant assumption that God is willing to overlook small sinning so long as we avoid the 'big' sins so prevalent in our culture, that if we do most things correctly we can indulge in a few sins without damage. I am talking about the enjoyment of secret, private sins of the heart. While there should be no discontinuity between our private lives and our public ones, integrity of character is shredded, creating the occasion for darkness to become prevalent, though not universally so. Little sins often lead to callousness that mutates into larger ones!

Fifth, it is important that we do not equate walking in the Spirit with the mere accumulation of biblical knowledge or think that attendance at meetings will automatically lift us spiritually. Without the submission of our hearts, meaning the focusing of our affections on the Lord, such disciplines can become the occasion for spiritual pride and arrogance, a false, deceptive sense that we are pleasing to God. Such mechanical notions, meaning the merely doing of things and the avoidance of others, may be the occasion for indwelling sin to grip our souls. Spirituality has more to do with our heart-affection for God through Christ than with a list of pious activities.

Sixth, indwelling sin, the twistedness of our inner being revealed through the thoughts and intents of our hearts, the ground of subsequent action, is revealed to us in our failure to see sin from a divine perspective. We

know that we are out of step with the mind and will of
God when we fail to repent. Why is it that we handle
the grievousness of our sinning, by pretending that it is
not all that serious? Why do we not intuitively recognize
that any act or thought contrary to the character of God,
His holiness and righteousness, is of infinite proportion
because the gravity of the wrong is proportionate to the
person wronged? By our failure to repent, we are opening
ourselves to greater error!

Seventh, our struggle with the remnants of sin's once
universal hold on our lives, what is often called indwelling
sin, is often limited to the immediate symptoms and
consequences, not its root cause. If we concentrate on the
pain that sin has brought, the wounding of the conscience
or the damage done to others, without addressing the root
cause, resolution is impossible since behavior is only the
manifestation of a serious problem and not the cause. The
quest for immediate relief from sin may be an obstacle to its
defeat unless we learn from it and search out its deeper cause.

An Appropriate Illustration: The 'Forest' Metaphor

To help us to understand the meaning of indwelling sin,
let me return to the metaphor of a forest. We argued in
the previous chapter that if we could look at our lives
before the intrusion of the life-changing grace, as if flying
in an aircraft at 10,000 feet, what we would see below
is a tangle of unmitigated trees, weeds, and vines. Our
lives were characterized by involuntary sinfulness and
rebellious unbelief. However, should you fly over your life
after entering into the redemption that is in Christ Jesus,
you would observe some vast changes in the topography.
Yes, there would still be trees, weeds, and vines, but you
would observe something else; you would see vast areas
in the forest where many trees (read sinful actions and

unbelief) had been uprooted, the weeds and vines pulled up. The dominion of sin, its total sway over your life has ended forever, and what remains for us to deal with is what is beyond the clearings in the 'forest.'

We call the remainders in the forest indwelling sin or our besetting sins. The grace and mercy of God through the cross-work of Christ, and its redemptive application by the Spirit, has changed the contours of our forest. The struggle will be with us until our identity with Christ is experientially completed, the forest destroyed, with our new and resurrected bodies. John stated the thought this way: 'Beloved, now are we children of God, and it has not appeared as yet what we shall be. We know that when He appears, we shall be like Him, for we shall see Him just as He is' (1 John 3:2). As we walk toward increased maturity, while in possession of an inadmissible increase of righteousness, since we are 'in Christ,' we will discover new trees, weeds, and vines that require uprooting. Growth in our spiritual lives is simply widening the clearings in our 'forest.'

THE DUTY TO DEAL WITH SIN'S PRESENCE

What, then, is our duty to the trees that remain in our 'forest'? It is the responsibility and privilege of every believer to work at cutting the 'trees' out of the 'forest,' rooting up the 'weeds' and 'cutting limbs' off the remaining trees that cannot be immediately eliminated from our lives. It is to widen the clearings in the forest of what dishonors God in our lives, to continue the reclamation of our lives, to gain greater freedom over the sin that so easily besets all of us. The duty as well as the instructions for its accomplishment are found in the texts of Scripture. Paul puts it this way in Romans 8:13: '... if you are living according to the flesh [here the meaning is a selfish lifestyle] you must die [here the idea is a fruitless life], but if by the Spirit you are putting to death the deeds of the body, you shall live.' If the believer does not struggle with the remainders of sin's influence (called 'the flesh'), this exhortation would not make sense. Paul told us in Romans 6:12: '... do not let sin reign in your moral body to obey its lusts,' clearly indicating that sin's grip in an existing sense has not been defeated. Why else would he instruct us in this manner?

DISCUSSION QUESTIONS

1. How has this chapter helped you to understand the fact that you have areas in your faith-walk where the light of the transforming gospel is not as bright as in some other areas?

2. If the truth of sin's complete dominion was ended forever, does this insight give you encouragement in your struggles? How does the struggle with the remnants of sin give you assurance that you are a child of God?

3. What is your duty in regard to the remnants of sin in your life? Do we grow in our righteous standing before God or do we grow in its application in our daily walk with God? Does our sanctification increase or does our experience of our completed sanctification, called maturity, increase?

4. What are some of the trees, weeds, and vines that have been uprooted in the forest of your life since you came to know Christ and His transforming power?

5. What are some of the trees, weeds, and vines that remain in your life and that you wish would be uprooted?

14

SOME GENERAL PRINCIPLES
IN DEALING WITH
INSTANCES OF SINFULNESS IN OUR LIVES

In our study, among a variety of other things, I have argued that there are two components of the spiritual life. The first is positive in nature; those actions or routines that promote the increase of spiritual health. The second, the one before us, is negative, corrective measures that are aimed at putting to death the manifestation of sinful attitudes and responses, as well as overt actions, that reflect the fact that redemption through Christ does not put an end to the struggle with sin. In fact, walking with God increases our awareness of the terrible cost of conceding to the beckoning solicitations of the trees, weeds, and vines that exist on the edges of the clearings in our forest.

For the sake of a helpful verse that capsulizes the importance of addressing sin in our lives, I have chosen as a summarizing text Romans 8:12-13: 'So then, brethren, we are under obligation, not to the flesh, to live according to the flesh – for if you are living according to the flesh, you must die; but if by the Spirit you are putting to death the deeds of the body, you will live.' In regard to these verses, we can say several things.

First, freedom from the condemning power of sin does not imply that we are free to do as we please; freedom brings duty, not to win divine favor, but because it has been bestowed on us richly in Christ. It is the obligation of every believer to struggle with sinful propensities while we await their total destruction.

Second, the 'for' of verse 13 explains the reason for our obligation to deal with sin in our lives. A life characterized by the bent of the flesh, the sin nature, will bring disappointment when we stand before our Lord (1 Cor. 3:12-15), when we will see the fruitless manner of our lives spent in self-gratification. A life lived in submission to the bent of the Spirit will issue in eternal life. Paul implies that the 'flesh,' meaning fallen human nature, still exists and also that there is danger from it.

Third, the 'if' statement-construct of the verse indicates a fact from the perspective of the writer, not a mere possibility; it is assumed that a believer will struggle to minimize the impact of the remainders of sin's once universal dominance and that our struggle will have a wonderfully positive outcome.

Fourth, the 'you' in the verse is plural, meaning each and every believer, all of us. For those who live according to the flesh, those devoid of the Spirit, the end is not mere physical death or the presence of self-destructive behavior; it is eternal separation from God. However, those who walk in obedience to the Spirit, exuding the fruit of the Spirit's indwelling presence (Gal. 5:22-25), will find the path to the maturing manifestation of righteousness in and through our lives a wonderful delight, a benefit to others, and an abundant entrance into glory (2 Pet. 1:2-9).

Some Preliminary Thoughts

As we are about to address the issue of putting to death sin in our lives, we will make a few clarifying statements before continuing. First, I am not at all claiming that the struggle with sin can be brought to an end in this life; I am not suggesting that we can gain victory over all of our wayward thinking or the consequences of negative behavioral patterns. I am saying, however, that we can make significant progress by addressing sin in our lives. In the forest of our lives, sin still is present, though the deforestation project has commenced. We can uproot trees and remove troubling weeds and vines. The difficulty is that sin is deeply rooted within; it has many subterfuges, and the dimensions of it are immense. While we are working to subdue a particular sin in our lives, removing a particular tree, weed, or vine, several others are growing up behind us!

Second, experience has taught me that sin-issues are often not resolved, so much as they can be deprioritized. While we can address a particular context that finds us very susceptible to sinning, we have not gained victory of it necessarily; we have simply gained wisdom to spot the approach of a context and so avoided a negative, sinful reaction. What we have done is address a context, not address the underlying cause, and, as such, the real cause is not addressed, and it simply reappears in a new context. Deprioritizing a sinful response by learning how you fall prey is found in learning the common circumstances of its recurrence; however, it may be too large a problem at a particular juncture in your spiritual maturity. If a tree cannot be uprooted, it is wise to remove some of the branches!

Third, a serious endeavor to walk in the Spirit, meaning engagement in positive and negative activities to clear away the remaining trees, weeds, and vines, does not suggest that the manner of doing it is to disguise a serious problem with a denial of it or the hiding of it with a pious veneer; it is not to exhibit a righteous behavior to avoid the realities of a secret unrighteousness. Further, a frequently observed strategy to avoid dealing with a prevailing sin is in finding a diversion with the intent that busyness will make it go away. The way this ploy is often manifest is by becoming involved in good things like participation in a service project or even a Bible study. Good busyness may simply be an avoid-mechanism that will never address the real issues. Pretending is pretending! Another way of mishandling trees is the development of a quiet, sedate exterior that hides the troubled soul within. When the real you is not exposed to the light of the gospel, it can never be resolved.

TEMPTATION: THE CRUX AND ORIGIN OF SIN

Solicitation is the precipitating context of any action, though not the cause of it. The origin of an idea that we may entertain, resulting in some form of positive response or rejection comes from two sources: either from within ourselves, what our mind dwells upon, or what comes into our preview from outside of us. As such, what we find pleasant and beneficial will become the catalyst for any decision we make (the mind entertains information, the affections judge the propriety of the information, and the will enacts the judgment of the affections resulting in action).

The quality of the source-material our minds dwell upon is integral to our choices and subsequent actions. Since the topic in this section is dealing with or cutting out of our lives our gullibility to the wrong actions, it is imperative that we understand how sinful behavior becomes a reality in our lives. The obvious answer is that we fall to temptation. It can be argued that you and I cannot prevent temptation, but we can prevent its potentially ravaging consequences by being attentive to its encroachment. Martin Luther made the point succinctly when he said, 'You cannot prevent the birds from flying over your head, but you can prevent them from making a nest in your hair!' Did not Jesus say to us, 'Keep watching and praying that you do not enter into temptation ...' (Matt. 26:41)? Because temptation or solicitation precedes our reaction to it, whether embrace or rejection, it seems that we should explore the concept before we become more specific about actually dealing with sin in our lives: the trees, weeds, and vines.

First, the word 'temptation' has two meanings, one negative and the other positive, the distinction being in origin and motive. James 1:12-16 reveals this clearly because the same word is translated in two ways: temptation or trials. Again the issue of the translation choice has to do with origin and motive. When the word is translated as 'trials,' the origin is from God and the motive is the promotion of our maturity (1:2-4). Trials come from the Lord to deepen our prayer life (1:5-8), to help us gain perspective on life (1:10-11), and to prepare us for 'the crown of life' (1:12). Solicitations to evil involves any thought or act contrary to God's character and conduct (1:16-18). When the term has a negative connotation, as it does in Matthew 26:41, it means anything that has the force or efficacy to deceive the mind and seduce the heart of a person from obedience to Christ.

Second, the instruction in Matthew 26:41 is that we should be on our guard against entering into temptation, here used as solicitation to what is contrary to God's character. To 'enter' means to come into the sphere of its influence. Two ingredients turn temptation into sinful action: the perception of some kind of advantage and the entangling of our affections. We know that we are in a season of temptation when allurements, circumstances, and urgency, the thought of willing necessity, combine. James 1:14-15 tells us that temptation is the root in our personal desire for what is contrary to God (he calls it lust); desiring leads to enticement, enticement eventuates in sinful behavior, and sin leads to destruction.

Third, it is important to know when you are 'entering' into a sphere of temptation. Again, while you and I cannot prevent crazy and destructive thoughts, we can prevent them from coming to fruition! When a particular allurement becomes a singular focus that you cannot shake, however much you try, you should know that you are entering into the sphere of temptation. Remember, temptation is not sin; it is only its beckoning call. You do not have to succumb to it (sin is voluntary for the saint of God)! Further, you can know that you have entered into a season of temptation when a particular solicitation is appealing, when you find a particular action to your 'assured' advantage ('After all God wants you and me happy and fulfilled, bubbling with self-esteem' goes the logic!). Abraham thought self-protection was to his advantage (Gen. 12:10-20); as did David in regard to Bathsheba (2 Sam. 11:2-5); Hezekiah and his extension of years (2 Kings 20:1-6, 15-19); Jonah's refusal to preach to his nation's enemies (Jon. 4:1-2); Peter's prideful claim that he was above ever denying his Lord (Mark 14:27-30); and the acrimonious conflict between Euodia and Syntyche (Phil. 4:2). Also, be aware that when you experience a blessed day, a time of spiritual health, it may be the occasion for spiritual slumber that the devil can use to his advantage. Success may lead to self-confidence and a lack of spiritual watchfulness! Yesterday's triumph may lead to today's failure, if not handled properly.

Fourth, if watchfulness and prayer are the means of preventing temptation from being the occasion for sinning, are there some helpful instructions for nipping the 'flower' in the bud? When are we most liable to temptation? While we all differ, it is important that we become a student of ourselves; the master psychologist, the father of lies, the archenemy of our spiritual well-being, knows that when it comes to deterring us 'one size does not fit all.' He knows our weaknesses far better than we do and knows how and when to strike.

Some Action Steps

Be Aware. It seems that the first bulwark against the consequences of temptation is to be attentive to the presence of temptation. Did not Jesus instruct us, 'Keep watching and praying that you do not enter into temptation' (Matt. 26:41)? Have we not all sung to our children, of course accompanied with proper gesturing, 'O, be careful little eyes what you see, be careful little ears what you hear, be careful little hands what you do, be careful little feet where you go ... '? Actions are the fruit of thoughts, so it is imperative to be attentive to what ideas we allow ourselves to entertain.

Act Quickly. The longer you entertain an alien idea the greater the possibility that damage will result. You and I, with time and upon reflection, can come up with a litany of arguments for any course of action we want to pursue. When something is clearly contrary to the character of God, we need to remind ourselves that it will never pay positive dividends, but it will only create a callousness over a behavior that justifies its embrace and makes it easy to condone repeatedly. When you enter into a season of temptation, it is not time to be complacent!

Pause to Pray. When confronted with any temptation, immediate refocusing is crucial. When we turn to the Lord in prayer, what we are doing is not only turning away from what could lead to destruction, we are turning to the solution. The fundamental issue is that our choices are based on what we value. By humbling ourselves before the Lord, we are focusing on One who is greater, higher, and more beautiful than what we would otherwise contemplate. The writer to the Hebrews tells us that we have a high priest, exalted in the heavens, to whom we can turn to reorient our thoughts and find sustaining strength. 'For we do not have a high priest who cannot sympathize with our weakness, but One who has been tempted in all things as we are, yet without sin. Let us therefore draw near with confidence to the throne of grace, so that we may receive mercy and find grace to help in time of need' (4:15-16).

Remember That You Are Precious to God. When we are tempted in some way or another, we suffer from the potential of momentary proper-attention disorder; if God is the most glorious, most merciful, and most caring of all, to not think of Him, but to allow ourselves to be enamored by lesser things, is utter senility. With the alluring possibility of lesser pleasures before us, it is the time to think of greater pleasures, the delight and commitment that God has revealed to us in the giving of the Lord Jesus. Did not Paul say to us, 'He who did not spare His own Son, but delivered Him over for us all, how will He not also with Him freely give us all things?' (Rom. 8:32). The argument in the verse is simply the assurance of a lesser based on the gift of something far greater. If God gave us life through the death of the Lord Jesus Christ, if Christ in obedience to the will of God assumed humanity so as to identify with us to become our penalty paid, the curse of sin removed by a payment to divine justice for us, it seems more than reasonable to conclude that thinking of the wonder and beauty of Jesus would make tempting lesser gains appear to us unacceptable. When 'seeming' advantage comes in the form of temptation, it would be helpful to focus upon the One who loves us more deeply than you and I can ever conceive. Think about what Peter tells us: 'and He Himself bore our sins in His own body on the cross, that we might die to sin and live to righteousness; for by His wounds you were healed. For you were continually straying like sheep, but now you have returned to the Shepherd and Guardian of your souls' (1 Pet. 2:24-25).

Think of the Damage of Concession. Knowing that temptation is the first step to bad choices, and that bad choices result in inappropriate behavior on our part, it would be extremely helpful to pause and think of the possible consequences to yourself, to your family, and to others outside of your family. Sin has never paid a positive dividend in the history of mankind from the instance of the first sin of the human race (Gen. 3), so sober reflection on implications would prove helpful in ending things at the temptation stage. If a husband or wife, you should think of the hurt inflicted on a loved one that eventual disclosure will cause. If a parent, think of the implications of momentary pleasures on your children when your broken promises are revealed. If all of us would only pause and think beyond the immediate to the consequences, it would greatly help. Confession is proper and right, but the damage can last for generations!

Run. There is an old adage that goes something like this: 'It is no fool that is willing to lose a battle in order to win a war.' What I am suggesting is that there are some temptations that are so potent that the best we might be capable of is not to formulate some resolve or resistance, but simply to walk away, to escape. Using the metaphor of the forest, some trees that remain in our lives may prove so strong that when they appear it is impossible to cut them down, or even to remove some of the branches; in such cases, it is best to simply end the encounter in retreat. Some people endure habits and addictions that are imposing; in such cases it is best to escape from them and hope that, with growth in the Lord, a different approach can be taken. If fascinated by pornography, it would be a good strategy to avoid certain media venues or social circles. If troubled by billboards along a route you take to work that create lustful thoughts, perhaps another avenue would be wise. If you get irritated by pushy drivers that speed past you and abruptly cut in to avoid long lines, causing you discomfort and stress, perhaps it would be best to allow a lot more time for travel to compensate for the rudeness of others. The list can be endless. My point is that we should speedily do something to stop the progress of temptation before it becomes detrimental to our spiritual health and that of others.

DISCUSSION QUESTIONS

1. What ways do you find yourself putting on a veneer of righteousness when it is a mask to hide your failure?

2. What are some areas in your life where you most struggle with temptation? If you are married, where would you say you struggle as a couple? As a single adult?

3. Why do you think you are more susceptible to a particular temptation rather than others? Is there something in your family history, events of childhood, severe instances of disappointment or betrayal?

4. How has the entertainment of temptation hampered your spiritual growth, your relationship to others, even family harmony?

5. What mechanisms or techniques have you found helpful in dealing with temptation so as to avoid its fruition?

6. Why do you think it is so hard for us to learn that temptation is dangerous, never leading to good outcomes if not handled correctly?

7. If being tempted is not itself sinful, what makes it so?

15

A Specific Approach

in Dealing with
Sinful Instances in our Lives

The promotion of a maturing manifestation of redemptive realities in our daily lives (the wonder of divine grace, the payment of the guilt of sin by Christ's atoning mercies, the possession of eternal life through the gift of the Holy Spirit who has cried aloud in our hearts 'Abba Father,' our adoption into the family of God, the gift of hope even in a blighted world) is the cumulative goal through the chapters in this book. The spiritual life is about nurturing within and exuding outwardly our righteous standing before God that we have found so transforming in our lives. We have been placed in Christ by the redemptive work of the Holy Spirit. Paul states it this way, God 'has blessed us with every spiritual blessing ... in Christ' (Eph. 1:3). You and I have been granted divine righteousness and, therefore, we have a complete and perfect standing before God. Since His righteousness, imputed to us through Christ, can neither increase nor decrease, the point for each of us is to seek ways to reveal it in and through our lives, our goal now being conformity to Him so as to reveal Him to others. For the Christian, our motive for spiritual development is not to gain something that we do not already possess, nor is it to keep what we have been

given as though we are motivated by fear that God would
fail in His promise. Our fundamental motive for maturing
the manifestation of righteousness in and through us is
gratitude, gratitude to God for the unspeakable gift of
forgiveness and the transforming power of His grace.

We come now to ask a very serious and fundamental
question: how are we to put Romans 8:13 into practice?
How can you and I go about 'putting to death the deeds of
the flesh?' When you and I struggle with an oft-prevailing
sin in our lives, when we encounter a remaining 'tree,
weed, or vine' in our lives, perhaps becoming aware of
it through the bitter fruit it produces, causing heartbreak
to others and disappointment in ourselves, how can we
either loosen its grip by removing some of the branches
or cutting it down completely?

The foremost, and most obvious, place to start is with
the realization that we have a struggle with sin. Clearings
are in the forest but 'trees, weeds, and vines' remain to
be uprooted if we are to mature in the manifestation of
the true life of God. Assuming that God reveals a short-
coming in your life, quite often through the pain of its
consequences, how can it be addressed? A second, all-
important question is this: are you willing to be willing to
deal it a death blow, or does it remain so deeply ingrained
that you have an addiction to it, finding pleasure in it?

SOME GENERAL ACTION STEPS

When 'sin crouches at the door' of your life, the tendency
for all of us is to only see the immediate benefit of an
action, massing a series of justifications instantly, but not
the consequences of a particular action. For example,
pause and think about the consequences of allowing
a temptation to come to fruition. Can a lie destroy a
family's trust? Think for a moment of the shame of a

momentary illicit pleasure, when it is revealed. Think about the turmoil that it will bring to those who love and depend on you. Is there no obligation to those with whom we have been entrusted to care and nurture?

I did not have a nurturing, loving father, most likely attributable to the difficulties and tragedies that he experienced. He suffered the loss of his mother as a child, endured a cruel stepmother, and the pain of the death of his father as a pre-teen. Life with his grandparents had a tragic moment when his grandfather committed suicide in his presence. The need to provide for his grandmother and sister thereafter, brought an end to whatever educational advantage he might have gained. My father had a hard life and he duplicated it by how he treated my mother and his children. The vicious cycle was broken for me through the graciousness and love of several men that came into my life in my early years: a neighbor through whom I came to hear of Jesus, a man that gave me a job as I had to make my way through college, a teacher in college and graduate education that became my mentor for life, and a father-in-law that showed me how to be a husband and what a Christian family looks like. I have been the recipient of the kindness and sacrifice of four individuals to whom I owe a great debt. I often think that if I dishonor my Lord, my family, my wife on some anvil of pleasure unwarranted by the Scriptures, I will need to go to them and tell them that I have failed, that I treated all that they gave me as trite and unimportant. The embarrassment of admitting such things to those who have given me so very much has proven helpful in my choice-making. I so deeply appreciate what they did for me and when I think of the shame of telling them they had invested unwisely in my life, it has been a deterrent.

Another safeguard against the flowering of temptation is to pause and think of your Savior and the wonder of

His generosity to you. It seems that, when we decide upon any particular course of action, we are saying that what we choose is superior at the moment to the quality and benefit of all other options. In the case of inappropriate behavior that disobedience to God is to our greater benefit. Pause for a moment to consider what such a course of action would say about one who has shed abroad in your heart infinite kindness and mercy. Fill your mind with texts of Holy Scripture that remind you of God's great love. Remember, for example, the words of the writer to the Hebrews, '... we do not have a high priest who cannot sympathize with our weaknesses, but One who has been tempted in all things as *we are, yet* without sin. Therefore, let us draw near with confidence to the throne of grace, that we may receive mercy and find grace to help in time of need' (Heb. 4:15-16).

My point is simply this: stop and think, when you enter into temptation, of the ramifications of allowing it to bear fruit. Sin never pays a positive dividend. Think of the pain that it will bring to others, but, most importantly, to your Lord. The lyrics of 'Be Unto Your Name' by Robin Mark are worthy of our reflection in times of temptation.

> We are a moment You are forever
> Lord of the ages God before time
> We are a vapor You are eternal
> Love everlasting reigning on high.
>
> Holy, Holy Lord God Almighty
> Worthy is the Lamb who was slain
> Highest praises Honor and Glory
> Be unto Your name
> Be unto Your name.

We are the broken You are the healer
Jesus Redeemer Mighty to save
You are the love song we'll sing forever
Bowing before You blessing Your name.[1]

A Particular Action Step: Address the Root to Deal with the Fruit

If I were asked to describe a river, such as the Mississippi, my feeble attempt would be something like this. A river is composed of three distinct segments. The first is what we call the headwaters; this is composed of a number of tributes or streams that flow together, forming a greater volume of water than each of its several sources. The second is the meandering water of the several sources that flow for significant distance, being supplied by a number of smaller rivers as it progresses. The third component is the delta, an estuary in many cases. In the delta, the river culminates by flowing in an ocean (or in the case of the Mississippi, the Gulf of Mexico). My point is that sin occurs in the 'delta' of our 'rivers;' in its fruitful stage. However, the manifestation of sin is not to be confused with its cause (cause and effect are two distinct entities in most cases). The cause of a poor behavioral pattern is often hidden. Another way to express my thought is this: that which troubles us is often a fruit of something deeper that is triggering it. To make progress in our struggles, we must search out the underlying causes and deal with them. There are things hidden deep in your mind that you have purposefully hidden to avoid the pain of it. Reflection over time will generally make these known. This is where a skilled counselor can help.

The task before each of us is no easy one. It requires hard reflection and honesty. There are things hidden deep

---

1. https://genius.com/Robin-mark-be-unto-your-name-lyrics

in our minds that we have purposefully sequestered to avoid the pain of them, though they find manifestation in new contexts by reverting to old ways. Reflection over time will generally make these known. When things got hidden in our memory bank as children, we adopted regressive, sometimes combative, approaches to dealing with them (we ran, sulked, threw a temper tantrum yelling and screaming, hit a supposed aggressor, or hid in our rooms). That is often all a child can do; however, to employ the same mechanisms as an adult, for example in our marriages when we do not get our way, leads to greater problems in handling social relationships. In commending appropriate behavior as opposed to inappropriate conduct, the apostle Paul explained it this way: 'When I was a child, I used to speak like a child, think like a child, reason like a child; when I became a man, I did away with childish things' (1 Cor. 13:11). Experiences from the past, with accompanying coping strategies, can become default mechanisms in later life. Understanding the cause of an inappropriate response can aid in understanding our reactions and see them as immature.

Add to the forest image another; it is the 'river and the canoe' metaphor. When you discover a 'tree' in your forest, do not merely deal with it. If you can, try to figure out what triggers this course of action. Imagine the 'river' to be your life with the troubling issue as the delta, the place or instance of its manifestation, and the 'canoe' the means for searching out its cause. Get into your 'canoe' and paddle up the 'river' of your life and deal with the problem at the deepest cause you can discover. Problems are normally brought to our attention in the fruitful stage, not the causative stage. To root out a problem is to attack the root, not the fruit. It may be that you cannot canoe to the final cause of your liability or weakness, but the further you can paddle up the river, the closer you are in getting to the root cause.

Allow me to cite a personal example of what I am suggesting. Being a public figure as a pastor and teacher, at least to some minor extent, it is not uncommon for me to receive criticism. Often my wife would ask me, upon returning from my teaching post or a speaking engagement, how my day went. My typical reply was that it went well, only for her to discover later that it was not exactly the case. When confronted with the incomplete disclosure (let's call it what it was, a lie), I would apologize to her. However, one day, having stated the same apologetic plea, she responded by saying, 'You cannot be sorry because you have been saying the thing to me for years without changing your behavior.' I was shocked; first, because I knew she was right and, second, because I knew that I did not practice the sin of deception as a habit. However, why did I not answer my wife in an unsullied manner? I decided it was time to paddle my canoe from the 'delta,' the circumstance of my continued failure, up my 'river' to find the actual cause of the present unfaithfulness. I discovered that the real cause was a failure on my part to trust God for how my wife would react instead of trying to manipulate and control outcomes, hiding my frustrations rather than disclosing them to my best and most loyal friend who did nothing to be treated with half-truths. I found it to be a mechanism, hiding, to protect myself from the reaction of others. When I confessed the sin of fear and unwarranted control to spare myself of frustration in this particular instance, I not only found acceptance but comfort, as opposed to hostility, from my best friend in ways I have never experienced in our marriage. My sin was not lying – that was its manifestation, the escape mechanism – it was fear and distrust.

There are at least two important qualifications about what I am proposing before we proceed. **First,** description is not the same as prescription. Gaining greater insight into the root cause of combative, avoidance mechanisms, that are so much a part of you from past experience is not behavior-solving in and of itself. Knowledge is not a solution; it can only help you to understand inappropriate responses. It cannot correct them. Knowledge is important because there can be no change without it; however, the mechanism of change is willingness. Do you really want to change your behavior? If change is brought about by willingness, then how does one become willing to be willing to change? The answer is that you must have before you something you perceive as more important, beneficial, and beautiful than the results you get from other mechanisms. If sharp, bitter reactions to supposed threat bring only consequences you regret, then you should be willing to be willing to change. Knowledge helps us to understand, seeing possible errors. It is not sufficient for us alone to warrant change, we must find a substitute behavior-response. For you and me, that requires seeing ourselves in the light of the Holy Scriptures which inform us of grace and mercy in the Lord Jesus, making any choice out of conformity to His love for us inappropriate. Willingness to change comes from focusing on something greater and more beautiful than temporally successful, pain producing behavior; it is found in the beauty of the Lord Jesus who loves us and gave Himself up to death so that we could have true life (See Rev. 1:5).

Second, paddling the 'canoe' up the river from the sin-revealing, though not sin-causing, delta is not an easy task; in fact, it can be painful because you are confronting methods rooted in experience and validated with time, though they are destructive. You may not be able to find the root cause on the first, or second, 'trips,' but go as far as you can. This is where a true friend may be of help; as you talk an issue through with someone you often can gain insight for yourself in the process. Obviously, prayer and Scripture input are important as you take the journey. If you approach a 'tree' remaining in the once unmitigated forest of your life, you may find removing it too difficult (perhaps one that is a lifetime project), but you can remove some of the branches, lessening the impact of the tree on you and others. Some trees may be so stubborn that the best thing to do is avoid the tree entirely, not try to handle it, simply avoiding the circumstance, praying that with time and increased maturity you can address it (these we call 'besetting sins').

SOME PRACTICAL CHALLENGES

I want to conclude with some practical challenges. Because complexity complicates and simplicity simplifies, take on only one or two trees at a time and address them. Too many 'trees' leads to frustration and defeat; too many 'canoe' rides in the 'river' of your life makes for frustration. Remember that walking with God is a journey; it is a marathon, not a sprint; it takes time and training called discipline. Reflect on the advice of the writer to the Hebrews who described our task as a process. '... solid food is for the mature, who because of practice have their senses trained to discern good and evil' (Heb. 5:14). It takes time to be trained!

As an individual, pick a 'tree' and work on it. Search out its roots (the original cause), learn the circumstances of its troubling presence, fight against it with prayer, Bible reading, good company, and resolve. Always be mindful that change comes through focusing on this more beautiful than temporal alleviations of stressfulness.

If you are married, pick a tree as a couple and work on it together. What would you say is a serious obstacle in the health of your marriage? Discuss it, find out how it got started in the first place, search for ways to minimalize its impact, and hold each other accountable.

Relative to your workplace, pick a tree that needs addressing.

DISCUSSION QUESTIONS:

1. As you look back across your life, what 'trees' seemed to more readily disappear than others? Describe the fallen trees and uprooted vines and weeds that came almost immediately with redemption.

2. Can you name a couple of 'trees' that seem impossible to uproot, weeds and vines that just will not go away?

3. Where have you found the most practical help in dealing with 'trees, weeds, and vines' in your life? What lessons have you learned that might help others?

4. What would you say is the biggest 'tree' in your life right now? Are you willing to take a 'canoe ride'?

5. If you are married, what would you say, as a serious and godly couple, is the 'tree' you would like to fall in the forest?

Conclusion

The topic that I have chosen to consider in this brief work has not been an easy endeavor to execute. There are several reasons for this in my judgment. Perhaps foremost of these is that the subject, if considered with any degree of the seriousness that merits the discussion, can prove unsettling (improvement requires realization which is not always pleasant). Allow me to cite several causes for the possible disturbance of our tranquility.

First, and as stated previously, the wonder of divine redemption – the sheer and expected joy of the experience of having become acceptable, declared acquitted of all our wrong doings by a holy and just God; the encounter with a far more transcendent realm of existence that we had never realized existed with such magnificence and now revealed to us through the incarnation of Jesus Christ; and the gift of the life of God within each of us through the indwelling presence of the Holy Spirit, the life that Jesus purchased for us through His atoning, substitutionary sacrifice – has not solved all our problems; in fact, the experience of spiritual birth has actually created some.

You may have been told, as I was when introduced to the benefits of the Christian faith, that my struggles and uncertainties would be greatly abated; yet, it seems to me that what I heard and what was meant was proper, but not nuanced (I am willing to say that those who were so kind in bringing to me the words, works, and claims of Jesus simply were doing the best with their time, talents, and experience they possessed. I am grateful for every one of them).

Second, we are all reticent to deal with change unless it reaches a crisis. The failure to deal with personal defects in our character, whether it be thoughts, attitudes, or actions, is often found in the perception that tolerance is less painful and disruptive than the effort to secure a remedy. Such is easily understandable, though perhaps not justifiable. We all find alteration in our default strategies so intrenched that it is hard to alter our behavior; admittedly it is time consuming and painful (who among us finds it effortless to face our shortcomings?).

Perhaps the greatest obstacle, though some behaviors have become so commonplace that they have become habits (a habit is a routine that has become a natural go-to-thing without thought of consequences), is our unwillingness to change. In such instances, the behavior is often a method of self-justifying our response to either an undesired confrontation or some emotional frustration. Simply put, we all look for reasons, call them justifications, for not changing our attitudes and actions. Perhaps a common way of justifying an inappropriate response is the perception that the actions of others deserve and demand it. This is a case of projecting onto others the cause of our sinful response (Jesus talked to us about judgmentalism when He used the illustration of the speck-and-beam image [Matt. 7:2-5]; what bothers us in others causing us to be sensitive toward them may be what bothers us about ourselves).

Third, and I alluded to this above, entering into the life of Christ is a joyful reality that is beyond our abilities to articulate, though redemption is a taste of it, creating an enduring appetite or relish for more of it. Nevertheless, walking in Christ, being led by the Spirit, is not as easy at times. Redemption is a work of God, ours merely to receive because it is the placement of the divine by the divine in our very existence (finite causation, however potent, cannot cause the infinite). However, sanctification, while ultimately assured by divine promise (Rom. 8:28), is a process, not an instantaneous happening, as in the experience of the life of God infused in the indwelling of the Holy Spirit.

Being a process that is progressive in the realm of spiritual growth, time and activity that promote improvement are required. You and I live in a culture of the instantaneous fulfillment of many of our needs and wants; the enormous wealth in the general culture has not only made us impatient, but always in a hurry, in the quest for one accomplishment after another. When it comes to the process whereby we grow toward spiritual maturity, haste is an archenemy. As the stately oak began as a mere twig in the ground and its maturation process was indiscernible to the naked eye (growth only with time-lapse photography), so it is with Christlikeness. Because spiritual growth requires time and discipline, the endeavor requires tenacity and perseverance ('... the mature, who have their senses trained to discern good and evil' [Heb. 5:14]). The habits of Bible reading, prayer, and our gathering together with other believers for worship and mutual strengthening require both frequency and constancy. Further, God's sculpturing mercies come to all of us through a variety of happenings, some pleasant and some not, some of our own doing and some not, that transpire over decades.

Fourth, the strength of the believer in Christ, one who has become the recipient of God's mercies in granting us a complete and secure redemption, is the gift of the enabling, guiding, and comforting ministries of the Holy Spirit. As we have indicated, the dominating attribute of God, as it relates to the origin and cause of divine forgiveness, is the unmerited, uncaused, and under-appreciated-at-times love of God the Father. This great love of the Father was revealed to us through the incarnation of the Son of God and procured for each of us by His victory over death when He became our sin substitute on Calvary's tree (proved by His resurrection on Easter morning!).

What Jesus purchased in His atoning death was eternal life, the gift of the Holy Spirit. The Spirit is the love of God the Father – who because of Christ's sacrifice is both just and the justifier of those who place their trust in Him (Rom. 3:26) – now in the possession of every believer (Rom. 8:9). The importance of this insight is that the Spirit is the sanctifier, who by virtue of His residence within us, is producing the fruits of the Spirit and negating the 'desires and passions of the flesh' (Gal. 5:19-23).

How does the Spirit accomplish His maturation of the believer, their growth in grace? While there are many avenues for its accomplishment, the primary one explained in this book is *willingness*. The Spirit works with us 'to will and do.' How does He make us willing? While coercion or supernatural intervention is not beyond His options in guiding, teaching and protecting His children, His every day, or normal, method is to work in us through the input of good, wholesome, godly thoughts. I am reminded of the provisions of the New Covenant. While the Old Covenant was written in stone to be observed, being external, the New Covenant promises are written within, a consequence of the indwelling Spirit. 'Behold, days are coming, says the Lord, when I will effect a New Covenant … I will put my laws in their minds and write them on their hearts' (Heb. 8:8-10). This is the very point where the disciplines we have enumerated are crucial because they are the means of putting good ideas in our mind, reminding us of all that is consistent with the indwelling Spirit. The issue for us is our personal willingness to enter into a life-long journey, through the disciplines of godliness, to 'grow in grace and knowledge of our Lord and Savior Jesus Christ' (2 Pet. 3:18).

The intent of my writing this book, an attempt to conceptualize the spiritual life, was to resist the pendant to overstate the case for progress, promising more than can actually be delivered, which can lead to frustration, apathy, and despondency when desires do not become realities. Yet I also aimed to show that spiritual progress is not only possible; it can be, and actually is, a reality (hopefully the book has been a practical encouragement to you along those lines). How can anyone not grow in their faith-walk when they avail themselves of the means of grace: God's Word, God's people, God's church and its many offices? Let me take a moment to summarize what I have sought to present in this book.

1. The beginning point in the discussion of the spiritual life is with God and His purposes because 'from Him, and through Him, and to Him are all things' (Rom. 11:36). Walking with God is about God, His interests. God's ultimate goal is the recognition of His worth and praise.

2. To increase His recognition and adoration, God determined to reach beyond Himself and create an extension of Himself. Our triune God created all that

we see so that it would accrue to Him glory by the recognition of His power, beauty, and providential and superintending benevolence.

3. Sadly, the creation, and primarily humanity, the ultimate of His creative power, failed in its duties, though being wonderfully supplied for success. Consequentially all of His creation from the animal kingdom, to the earth itself, and the heavens also, failed. Although He desired a world to praise Him, the earth chose rebellion and devastation.

4. Though at that point it appeared that God's desire was stymied, He began a wonderful reclamation work that has extended through the centuries. He is gathering a new people to praise Him, composed of myriads and myriads, in a new creation (Rev. 21:2-4).

5. The method of gathering a new people is redemption – anticipated in the Old Testament Scriptures, revealed in the Gospels, progressively fulfilled in the Acts and Epistles and subsequent centuries, and which will be completed when the last person is gathered into His kingdom, which will then commence eternity, God dwelling forever amid the praises of an adoring, thankful people.

6. Because I have found significant direction in the art of growing in the graces of Christ through the reading of those in the past who were much more experienced in the endeavor than I, finding a treasury of helps encased in simplicity, depth, and clarity, I thought it worthy of the effort in writing a summary of others' ideas. In essence those of a few centuries past thought in terms

of a double strategy: first, those activities that promote the emergence of good ideas such as regularity in Bible reading, prayer, church involvement including formal instruction, hearing of sermons, and participation in the Lord's Table, to name a few; and, second, clues to walking with God in the uprooting of destructive thoughts and actions.

As this study closes, I would like to offer some advice in the words of a poem written by John H. Sammis (1846–1919), later set to music by Daniel Towner (1850–1919), that directs our hearts to the Lord Jesus; it is entitled *Trust and Obey*.[1] It seems to me, though the mechanics of the two words required delineation, that the title captures what I have sought to explain – TRUST and OBEY!

When we walk with the Lord
In the light of His Word,
What a glory He sheds on our way;
While we do His good will,
He abides with us still,
And with all who will trust and obey.

Not a shadow can rise,
Not a cloud in the skies,
But His smile quickly drives it away;
Not a doubt or a fear,
Not a sigh or a tear,
Can abide while we trust and obey.

Not a burden we bear,
Not a sorrow we share,
But our toil He doth richly repay;

---

1. The entire poem is found in *Gospel Hymns of the Faith* (Grand Rapids: Zondervan Corporation, 1974), 261.

Not a grief or a loss,
Not a frown or a cross,
But is blest if we trust and obey.

But we never can prove,
The delights of His love,
Until all on the altar we lay;
For the favour He shows,
And the joy He bestows,
Are for them who will trust and obey.

Refrain:
Trust and obey,
For there's no other way
To be happy in Jesus,
But to trust and obey.

BIBLIOGRAPHY

The sources listed here are those that have profoundly shaped my journey in understanding what it means to nourish a healthy walk with God: delighting in His presence, feeling the fresh breezes of intimacy, experiencing rebuke born of infinite love, instruction when I fall, and encouragement to pursue what is right and good, both privately and publicly. The list is not exhaustive by any means, but these offerings have helped me as I have sought to follow the Savior.

Bennett, Arthur (ed.). *The Valley of Decision: A collection of Puritan Prayers & Devotions*. Carlisle, PA: The Banner of Truth Trust, 1975. This volume is an unparalleled collection of spiritual insights, a wonderful source for focused thought on our God and His mercies.

Bridges, Jerry (1978), *The Pursuit of Holiness*, Colorado Springs: NavPress. This author is unusually helpful; this book is a classic in my judgment.

Bridges, Jerry (1988), *Trusting God: Even When Life Hurts*, Colorado Springs: NavPress.

Charnock, Stephen (1797), *The Existence and Attributes of God*. Reprint. Minneapolis: Klock & Klock (1977). Though an older work, it is a classic on the foundation of the spiritual life, which is knowing the character of God.

Edwards, Jonathan. 'Letter to Deborah Hathaway,' edited by George S. Claghorn (1998), Vol. 16:91-95. New Haven, CT: Yale University Press. Without a pastor, this young lady wrote to Edwards seeking spiritual advice in her walk with God; the reply is profoundly insightful for what Edwards says and does not say.

Edwards, Jonathan (rpt. 1986), *The Religious Affections*. Reprint. Carlisle, PA: Banner of Truth Trust. The critical edition of this work is found in the Yale edition of his collected writings, vol. 2, edited by Paul Ramsey. Excellent summaries of this work may be found in Gerald R. McDermott (1995). *Seeing God: Twelve Reliable Signs of True Spirituality*, Downers Grove, IL: InterVarsity Press; and Sam Storms (2007), *Signs of the Spirit: An Interpretation of Jonathan Edwards' Religious Affections*. Wheaton, IL: Crossway Books.

Edwards, Jonathan. *Resolutions*. Edited by George S. Claghorn (1998). Vol. 16. New Haven, CT: Yale University Press. The 'Resolutions' are Edwards' attempt, as a young man, to formulate and delineate the spiritual life for himself.

Edwards, Jonathan, *Standing in Grace*, reprint 2002. Morgan, PA: Soli Deo Gloria. The critical edition of this work is found in the Yale edition of his collected writings under the title, *Treatise on Grace*, vol. 21:153-97, edited by Sang Hyun Lee.
Murray, Andrew (1961), *Humility: The Beauty of Holiness*, London: Oliphant. This is a classic on the spiritual life and Christlikeness.

Owen, John, *The Works of John Owen*, edited by William H. Goold. 15 vols. reprint 1987, Carlisle, PA: Banner of Truth Trust. This is the standard collection of the writings of Owen. Individual titles by Owen have been recently published by a variety of publishers, among them Christian Focus, Crossway, and Multnomah Press. I found the following works of Owen most helpful and in this order: 'On Communion' (vol.1, 4-274); 'A treatise on the Dominion of Sin and Grace' (vol. 6, 500-60); 'On Indwelling Sin' (vol. 6, 154-322); 'On Temptation' (vol. 6, 88-150); 'On Grace and Duty of Being Spiritually Minded' (vol. 7:262-497); 'On Mortification' (vol. 6, 1-86); and 'On the Holy Spirit' (vol. 3, 366-651). A wonderful summary of Owen's understanding of the spiritual life is Sinclair B. Ferguson (1987), *John Owen on the Christian Life*, Carlisle, PA: Banner of Truth Trust.

Packer, J. I. (1990), A *Quest for Godliness: The Puritan Vision of the Christian Life*, Wheaton, IL: Crossway Books. This is an excellent synopsis of a reformed grasp of the spiritual life.

Packer, J. I. (1973), *Knowing God*, Downers Grove, IL: InterVarsity Press. The author writes with a biblical-centeredness and insight that is truly rare.

Ryle, J. C. (n.d.), *Holiness: Its Nature, Hindrances, Difficulties, and Roots*, Westwood, NJ: Fleming H. Revell Co. This is another classic; well-worth a careful, prayerful reading.
Tozer, A. W. (1961), *A Knowledge of the Holy*, New York: Harper Row. This is another classic as the author is deeply insightful.

Whitney, Donald S. (1991), *Spiritual Disciplines for the Christian Life*, Colorado Springs, Co: NavPress. I have found the works of this author to be deeply practical and applicational.

Christian Focus Publications

Our mission statement —

STAYING FAITHFUL

In dependence upon God we seek to impact the world through literature faithful to His infallible Word, the Bible. Our aim is to ensure that the Lord Jesus Christ is presented as the only hope to obtain forgiveness of sin, live a useful life and look forward to heaven with Him.

Our books are published in four imprints:

CHRISTIAN
FOCUS

Popular works including biographies, commentaries, basic doctrine and Christian living.

CHRISTIAN
HERITAGE

Books representing some of the best material from the rich heritage of the church.

MENTOR

Books written at a level suitable for Bible College and seminary students, pastors, and other serious readers. The imprint includes commentaries, doctrinal studies, examination of current issues and church history.

CF4•K

Children's books for quality Bible teaching and for all age groups: Sunday school curriculum, puzzle and activity books; personal and family devotional titles, biographies and inspirational stories — because you are never too young to know Jesus!

Christian Focus Publications Ltd,
Geanies House, Fearn, Ross-shire,
IV20 1TW, Scotland, United Kingdom.
www.christianfocus.com
blog.christianfocus.com